The lipstick gospel

By Stephanie May Wilson

THE LIPSTICK GOSPEL
Published by For Every Story, LLC.
foreverystory.com

Copyright © 2014 Stephanie May Wilson
stephaniemaywilson.com

Design by Carl Wilson
carlswilson.com

Interior photograph by Kailey Dickerson

All Scripture quotations are taken from the Holy Bible, New International Version®, NIV®, Copyright © 1973, 1978, 1984, by International Bible Society.

"The Stand" written by Joel Houston
Copyright © 2005 Hillsong Music Publishing

ISBN: 978-0-6923-3692-2

Printed and distributed in collaboration with
On-Demand Publishing LLC (DBA Create Space).

First Edition 2014

for Kelsey & Michelle

Look at the nations and watch—
and be utterly amazed.
For I am going to do something in your days
that you would not believe,
even if you were told.

Habakkuk 1:5

INTRODUCTION

If you've ever traveled, you know there are two kinds of sojourners: those who travel with a map and those who don't.

Traveling without a map is the sexy way to travel. It's the makings for an adventure, going wherever the wind takes you, hopping on a train to a city whose name you can't pronounce, and meeting a quirky cast of characters along the way.

Then there's the other kind of traveler, the kind that can't stand this map-less, whimsical sort. These kinds of travelers really should run their own travel agencies with their attention to detail, library of guidebooks, and strategic plan for how they're going to see everything worth seeing in their country of choice.

These two groups exist in life too: the people with a map and those without. People with maps have five-year plans. They're your Type A personalities, head down, intent on getting from point A to point B. Then there are the more easygoing personality types, the wanderers, those who appreciate the scenic detour. They lag behind, nose deep in a scoop of gelato. Maybe they'll stay an extra week, or a month, who knows? They sure don't.

Either route can bring you to arduous places or lovely places. Sometimes you arrive at your destination and it looks nothing like you thought it would. And sometimes when you get lost, you stumble upon something more perfect than you could have found on your own.

I was a person with a plan, but I've never gotten to where I was going—not because I got lost, but because I was rerouted along the way.

Chapter 1: The Writing On The Mirror

"I'll be home in 15 minutes, are you guys leaving for the bar yet?" I shouted into my cell phone, trying to make my roommate hear me over the girls laughing in the background on her end.

"I don't know…we're leaving soon…just hurry!" I pressed down harder on the pedal. I knew I was cutting it close.

David Guetta was performing at a club in Denver that night, and some fraternity guy had rented a fleet of decked-out party buses to bring everyone to the event. All my friends were going, and at the last minute, hating the idea of being the only one left behind, I bought a ticket. *I'm so late, everyone is probably ready to go*, I thought, gripping the steering wheel tighter. *Hell, they're probably already drunk*. I had a lot of catching up to do.

The truth is that I didn't really want to go to the concert. I loved David Guetta (and still do), but I wasn't in the mood for a night out. My limbs felt heavy as I pictured the hassle of getting dressed up, of making small talk, of trying to have fun. What I *was* in the mood for was a weeklong nap and a pint of Ben and Jerry's, but I was hoping a night out might serve as a welcome vacation from the thoughts I'd been drowning in recently.

With my oversized workbag slung over my shoulder, I raced around the corner of the imposing, dollhouse-like mansion that was my sorority house. I sprinted up the wide stone steps, taking them two at a time. Then, ignoring the throngs of party-ready girls congregating in the front hall, I slipped through and bounded up to my room.

I tore through my closet and tossed options behind me, none of them quite fitting the bill—too fancy, too old, too stuffy, too ratty. Coming up empty, I peered into the hallway where girls were putting the final touches on their club-wear. *How do they do it?* I wondered, narrowing my eyes at their effortlessly stylish ensembles. They always looked like they'd just stepped off the cover of a magazine—no matter how hard I tried, I could never seem to pull that off. I shuffled back to my closet more convinced than ever that everything hanging inside was hideous.

Dammit! Why do I never have anything to wear?

Running out of time, I surveyed my options again and then selected a plain black dress, yanking it off the hanger, and slipping it over my head. It wasn't particularly cute, and the outfit was devoid of creativity, but it was the best I could find. If I did my hair and makeup with enough flair, I figured I could get away with the plain selection. I wasn't particularly skilled in the hair department either, but I had a secret weapon for that one. Carolyn, the president of our sorority, was an expert with a comb. I was convinced she could have teased any head of hair into submission. If I hurried, I knew she'd improve the situation.

Peering into the mirror in our bright community bathroom, I swiped on layer after layer of eyeliner and bronzer—to hell with subtlety! I squinted at my reflection, turning my face from side to side to examine my work. *I guess that'll have to do.* I took one last look in the mirror before giving up, and sprinted downstairs to bring my mop of blonde hair to the pro.

I flopped into Carolyn's desk chair that was pulled up to her dresser and peered into the large mirror she'd used to create a makeshift vanity. I held pieces of my hair obediently as she doused others with hairspray. She back-combed them ferociously—teasing them until they were matted, tangled, and actually had some volume.

Impatient, I checked the time on my phone. *Shit! How did it get so late?* I pictured my friends upstairs, grabbing their bags and taking pictures together—none of which I'd be in because I had taken too long to get ready. For the thousandth time that night, I wished I had better clothes, better makeup, better hair, better something—anything to make me feel like I could hold a candle to the women around me. Being surrounded by some of the most beautiful, confident, talented women on campus usually left me wishing I could be one of them instead of having to be me.

If I were a team captain in high school gym class, I'm fairly certain I would have picked myself last for my own team.

They say we are our own worst critics, but I was my own worst enemy. I criticized everything about myself, my clothes, my appearance, my personality, any imperfection my mean little thoughts could find. I'd speak up in a conversation, and then once my words were out, the diatribe would begin. *Why did you say that?* I'd ask myself. *You're so embarrassing. That was so dumb!*

But I wasn't ready to give up yet. I was convinced that with enough polish, duct-tape, and hard work, I could become the kind of person I was proud of. I was sure my life could feel as fulfilling on the inside as it looked on the outside. That night out was another chance to start over.

As Carolyn teased, and sprayed, and shaped my hair, I tried to distract myself. I looked around her room; books and magazines and photos and clothing were strewn everywhere. Her life seemed so fun to me—so wild and untamed and full of people who loved her. Her friendships seemed to seep into every nook and cranny, exploding with color and life and spilling onto the floor.

Even though we were in the same sorority, my friendships didn't feel like that. I thought being in a sorority meant living in a house full of best friends, and in some ways it did. But it didn't mean *best* friends. Not the kind I'd hoped to find, anyway. To me, best friendship meant you were safe to leave the room without knowing people were going to talk about you once you were gone. It meant you were free to be yourself without being criticized or made fun of. I had friends, certainly, but I felt frantic inside my friend group, trying to manage their opinions of me and scrambling to not be left behind.

I bounced in Carolyn's chair, my bare heels swinging hard against its metal legs. I was like a sprinter at the starting line, rigid and ready to bolt the second she gave my hair one last spritz of hairspray. Pre-gaming (getting drunk before the party) waits for no woman. And I was in desperate need of some liquid courage.

My eyes wandered down her huge mirror, taking in the photos and clippings and ticket stubs taped along the side. Just as I was about to look away, my eyes landed on a quote. It was in the top, right corner of the mirror, and I couldn't believe I'd missed it before.

It was written in lipstick in round, perfect letters.

"Look at the nations and watch—and be utterly amazed. For I am going to do something in your days that you would not believe, even if you were told."

In that instant, the world screeched to a halt. My eyes zoomed in on the words and everything else faded away, quiet and fuzzy in the background. My insides had gone cold and somehow warm all at the same time. That was it. That was the quote I wanted to define my life. I squeezed my eyes shut tight, trying to picture a life that was so good I wouldn't believe it even if I'd been told. I couldn't picture it, but I wanted to keep trying.

"What is that from?" I demanded.

"The Bible," Carolyn answered, almost embarrassed.

"Shut the hell up!"

the david guetta disaster

"Steph! We're leaving!" one of my roommates called a few minutes later from down the hall. I scooped up my coat and heels from Carolyn's bed, thanked her with a quick hug, and dashed down the stairs.

My friends and I slipped and slid our way up the hill toward The Goose, a bar near campus where the buses were waiting. The weather hadn't managed to muscle its way up past zero and our feet were freezing in our strappy stilettos. The Goose was always our bar of choice. The drinks were cheap and it was within stumbling distance from our house. Regardless of where the misadventures of the night took us, we always found our way back to The Goose.

The warm bar was a respite from the stinging mountain air. I was glad to be out of the uncharacteristically depressing Colorado weather, although it reflected my mood perfectly.

Lately, I'd begun to wonder if I was depressed, a label that had always frightened me with its severity. I felt listless and heavy. Nothing felt exciting and I cried more than I wanted to admit to anyone. My life looked great from the outside, I made sure of that. I was a journalism major and at the top of my class, I was in the best sorority on campus, and I went to all the best parties. But I rattled around inside my perfect life. My eyes looked like the windows of an abandoned house whose heat had stopped working years ago. I wasn't sure what made me come alive anymore; I hadn't felt truly happy in as long as I could remember. There was another small detail: I was nursing a seriously broken heart.

I repeated that Bible quote in my head again. I was really hoping it knew something I didn't.

Weaving through the masses of Guetta fans, I made a beeline for the bartender. I'd missed the pre-game entirely and did not want to go to the concert sober. I ordered two double whiskey Sprites (my friends' variation to the classic Whiskey Coke), and with a drink in each hand and both straws in my mouth I sucked them down before the buses arrived.

"They're here!" I heard the shout and looked around, realizing my friends were gone. I glanced out the window just in time to see the last of my roommates climbing onto a bus before it pulled away. Thankfully I spotted two familiar faces, friends from a sorority across campus. I weaved my way through the crowd before I lost them too, and the three of us boarded the last bus together.

The bus shook to the beat of the pulsing techno music. Finding a seat, I looked around at the faces of my fellow Guetta fans. Most of them were unfamiliar except for my two friends and a guy who had hooked up with almost every girl I knew; we had lost track of exactly how many. The bus rumbled down the highway and after a few minutes of laughing and yelling over the techno music, I caught his eye. He wobbled over to me—not an easy feat on a moving bus—just as I noticed I still wasn't up to everyone else's level of total inebriation.

Some guy on the bus had a crystal decanter full of Southern Comfort (which, now that I think about it, is such a strange thing to bring on a party bus), and so, quickly making friends,

I asked him for some. The bus cheered as I took gulp after gulp of the syrupy alcohol straight out of the decanter, only stopping long enough to take a sip of Red Bull to wash it down. (For the record, I *hate* Southern Comfort.)

But my chugging paid off, because that guy was now friendlier than ever. It may have been the outfit I'd cobbled together, or the makeup I'd slopped on my face, or my sudden surge of alcohol-sponsored confidence, but my cold insides felt just a little bit warmer in the glow of his attention. We made small talk for a few minutes—or whatever the drunk, party bus, screaming over techno music equivalent is—and then he pulled a small plastic bag of white powder out of his pocket, offering it to me.

Now I'm nothing of a drug connoisseur, but I recognized the white powder as Molly, a form of ecstasy that was getting pretty popular. He encouraged while I debated. I wasn't a habitual drug user, or a drug user at all. But something about the beat of the music and the deviousness of his smile had me wondering if maybe all of that was about to change.

I reached for the bag, ignoring the fact that I had no idea what to do with Molly (snort it? eat it? put it on your gums?). But just as my hand grazed the outside of the plastic, I locked eyes with my friend Jess. Jess had always been a good influence on me. She was fun, certainly, but smart. I could rely on her for good advice when I needed it. And in this moment, I needed it. Desperately.

In a sudden, surprising moment of clarity I stood up, almost knocking the bag out of his hand. I grabbed Jess's arm, pulled her aside, and whispered (to the best of my ability over the beat of the music), "Tell me not to do it."

Somewhere, deep below my SoCo-soaked brain I knew that I didn't want to. I knew I was in over my head. I knew that no matter how drunk I got, no matter how unhappy I was, ecstasy wasn't something I wanted to get acquainted with.

She tilted her head down just the littlest bit and stared me straight in the eyes.

"Don't do it."

So I didn't.

That was my last memory of the night.

The next day, the afternoon sun streamed through my bedroom windows, despite the best effort of my tightly drawn blackout shades. I rolled over groggily and that's when the first stab of pain zinged through my left side. Startled by the pain, I tried to sit up, but moving made it worse. My head began to throb with it. *Brain injury?* My muddled thoughts were frantic as my mind tried to wake up. Giving up on movement, I laid flat on my back and deduced that I'd either been hit by a bus and forgotten about it (a real possibility), or I was suffering from the hangover of a lifetime.

But hangovers don't usually leave bruises. What happened to me last night?

I tried to roll over again, wanting to bury my head under

my pillow away from the offensive sunlight. But the stabbing pain was insistent and serious, and I couldn't seem to bend my arm.

What is today? How did I get home? What happened?

Still drunk, I started to panic. I checked myself for all of the physical signs of sexual assault. I knew what to look for. I was the one who made freshmen go through this kind of training. But no, everything felt normal—everything except for my head, and my left arm.

My thoughts shifted to my own transgressions. *Who do I have to apologize to? Did I do something stupid? I don't think I did anything terrible last night...did I?* But I couldn't remember a thing, so I wasn't the best witness to testify to my behavior the night before. I like to call this the "moral hangover." It's just as serious as the real thing, if not more. It permeates your insides until every crevice of you is sick with guilt, shame, and embarrassment over whatever stupid things you did the night before. Of these, I was an expert.

As I scrambled for my phone, a distant memory became clearer of Jess there with me on the bus. I dialed her number, hoping she could fill in the details.

According to Jess, I took several more sips from the crystal decanter before I stumbled off the bus holding hands with the Molly guy. I tripped on the curb, and tried to regain my composure but it was too late. Molly guy, figuring I was more trouble than I was worth, walked off into the club without me. As if that wasn't humiliating enough, I grabbed Jess's arm, telling her I needed to use the restroom, and pulled her into an alley behind several cars. As I tried to stand up, I lost my balance, and fell hard onto the concrete—nothing breaking my fall except my arm, my head, and my makeshift toilet.

A bouncer finally spotted me and could see I wasn't in any shape to make memories with Guetta. He hailed me a cab, Jess helped me inside, and they watched as the taxi pulled away to drive me home. Little did the bouncer know, home was an hour away. The night was over before it even really started.

Nobody knew what happened to me at that point, but I must have been able to tell the cab driver my address, he must have gotten me home safely (85 dollars later), I must have put myself in pajamas and gotten into bed, and there I was. The left side of my body was scraped and bruised, speckled with little bits of gravel, and I was surprised (and not entirely sure) I hadn't broken anything. Everything ached, my hangover was debilitating, but it didn't hold a candle to my moral hangover. My life had gone from bad to worse in 12 hours, and I was mad.

I was mad at myself for going to the concert. I was mad that the night out did nothing to make me feel better. I was mad at myself for getting so out of control. I was mad that no matter how out of control I got, it never seemed to make me as happy as it made everyone around me. But more than being mad, I was scared. Drinking was such a normal thing for my friends and me. Blacking out from drinking too much was all in a weekend's work, and a party wasn't a party if someone didn't do something stupid. But last night was something altogether new.

As I lay there, my insides shaking from dehydration, I was genuinely scared. My mind flipped through a slideshow of all of the terrible things that almost happened the night before.

In my mind I kept seeing that guy pull the baggie of white powder out of his pocket, and I cringed as I remembered how close I was to taking it from him. I thought about the crystal decanter and wondered how much I'd actually had to drink. I thought about my fall and the fact that I could have gotten seriously hurt. And I thought about the cab driver—thank God he had been kind. Thank God he had taken me home.

Thank God.

This is what rock bottom must feel like, I thought to myself. And then, for the millionth time that week, my thoughts drifted to Kyle. I tried not to think about him, but I just couldn't help it. Without him I didn't know who I was anymore. Part of me wondered what I was actually living for.

Chapter 2: Butterflies Like Bumper Cars

Every once in awhile, there are those great loves. Sometimes they don't make sense, and they're never perfect, but they're so intoxicating that you tumble head over heels as deep into love as you're able to dive, swearing you'll never come up for air again. That's how I fell in love with Kyle.

Kyle was different from any guy I'd ever met—charming in a way that caught you off guard. He wasn't the first guy you'd notice in the room, not for the usual reasons anyway. But he was mesmerizing. He was funny and creative. He was the kind of person that gives off the air that he understands something wild and passionate about the world. The kind of person that makes you want to know his secret too.

As it usually happens, I didn't have any idea what Kyle would end up meaning to me when we met.

When we did meet, it took about four seconds for Kyle to ask me out, and about four seconds after that for me to decide I wanted to say no. I wasn't ready for a relationship, my heart was still tender from my last breakup; I was not looking for anything serious. I tried to say no, I gave it my best shot. But he persisted, and he made me laugh. So after a few minutes on the phone, I heard myself agreeing to go out on a date with him, despite my hesitations.

We went on that date, and then another, and then another. We explored corners of the city I'd never noticed before. He took me to restaurants I'd never heard of and ice-skating downtown. Our dates were always elaborate and always a surprise. He was the best at surprises, and more often than not, I'd come home to flowers or a present on my second floor balcony. I never found out how he got those up there…a ladder maybe?

We could talk for hours and never run out of things to say; that was my favorite part. He quickly became my best friend, bringing out my inner dreamer and adventurer. He understood me in a way nobody ever had before, and the way he looked at me made me believe I really might just be something special. But he still hadn't convinced me to date him.

My high school love had broken my heart, and I wasn't ready to open up again. I had a strict policy of dating as many guys as I could at once; there was less chance of getting hurt that way—less chance of falling in love.

But he didn't quit.

Kyle called me every night for six months before I agreed to be his girlfriend. We'd talk about everything, about our days, about who we wanted to be, and about our families and what life looked like as we were growing up. It became my favorite part of my day, snuggled in my bed with my phone pressed to my ear. He was just a few miles away, but this felt safer than being in person somehow. It was during these phone calls that Kyle created a space for himself in my heart.

One Friday night when we were both home from school, Kyle took me to dinner at a hole-in-the-wall restaurant a few miles from my parents' house. It's one of my favorite spots because it's an old, oaky bar, and most of the regulars ride motorcycles. It's a total dive, but it has a great view and a patio that is perfect for drinking beers on warm summer nights. I made a point of spending as many of my summer evenings there as possible. So that's where we were, sitting out back, eating tacos and drinking beer, talking about a thousand things like we always did. But after awhile his face grew serious and he told me why he'd wanted to go to dinner that night.

"Stephanie, we need to decide what we're doing here. I can't go on being in this middle ground with you. It's too painful," he grimaced.

"Come on," I started. We'd talked about this before, not directly necessarily, mostly because I'd dodge the subject every time I saw it coming.

But he stopped me. He was serious this time. I had to choose.

Logically I understood we couldn't go on just being friends like this. He was too much a part of my life to leave room for anyone else. He was the one I'd call whenever anything happened in my day; he was the first one I wanted to tell what I was thinking or feeling or wondering. He had become my best friend, a pillar in my life, and I couldn't stand to lose him. But I also could see how much this middle ground was hurting him. I had to either be his girlfriend or let him go.

So he hit me with the question directly, not letting me avoid it anymore.

"Stephanie, I want you to be mine. Will you please be my girlfriend?"

The sincerity of his words reverberated in my heart, bouncing off the walls and against the old scars and heartaches. I picked at my nail polish, avoiding his eyes. I still wasn't ready, or I didn't think I was. But he was my best friend, and I didn't want to picture my life without him. So I slowly raised my head, looked him in the eyes, and said yes.

That yes was all it took. That yes was like jumping into a tunnel slide at a water park—the water rushing me down the slick surface until I plunged into the pool below. I fell in love with him hard and fast and deeper than I knew I was capable of. I was head over heels. We spent every moment with each other, sleeping at his house together every night. I even had a toothbrush there. He bought it for me, a clear, plastic pink one. It sat in his toothbrush holder, right next to his blue one. We cooked together and dreamed together. We went on dates and adventures and did our homework together. Every moment was better with him in it, and when we were apart, I thought my heart was going to fall out with how intensely I missed him.

I felt like I'd arrived somehow—like my life had found the

missing piece. This man loved me and understood me, and made me believe I was actually good the way I was. I was smart and funny and interesting. I was going somewhere. I felt like I could take on the world when he was around. I felt like his love somehow made me taller, able to look the world in the eye and give it a firm handshake.

We weren't making any big plans for marriage, but we almost didn't have to. We had each found our person—our soul mate. We combined our lives as much as we could. His family was my family, my family was his. We gave each other the deepest parts of ourselves like a gift. We didn't even have to stop and wonder if it was wise or if we trusted each other. We did, unequivocally. "Here, take my whole life," I said without even a second thought. It was perfect.

But like most things, it also wasn't perfect.

No matter how hard we tried, his love couldn't compensate for all the other ways I was unhappy. No matter how much he tried to love me, my tank just never stayed full. I still didn't feel quite happy enough, quite secure enough, quite safe enough. He was my life raft and I was gripping on with both hands. But we were sinking, because I hadn't yet learned to swim, and he couldn't swim for both of us. Changes in his life and his family had zapped him of the joy and confidence I had fallen in love with, and after a year of dating, we realized the hole we were both in was too deep to climb out of together.

I didn't believe we were breaking up. He was a part of my life, a part of me. Our lives were so intertwined. I could not fathom what it would look like without him. I knew we were breaking up, but I thought it was temporary. It had to be temporary; this couldn't be real. When I pictured every scene in my life's future, he was there. I couldn't conceive of a reality where this could be permanent.

We talked around it for days, trying to solve problems one way or compensate in another. We tried to talk it through again, but it wasn't a problem between us. It was a problem with us each individually, and no compromises or conversations were going to fix it.

When we finally broke up, we sat in his car parked in front of my house. I knew it was over. We'd said the words. But I couldn't get out of the car. I couldn't watch him drive away, knowing he wasn't coming back. And so I sat there. We both did. We talked a little and cried a lot. But mostly we just sat there, the grief pushing against the floodgates, ready to overwhelm us at any moment.

Finally, having mustered up just an ounce of courage, and not knowing what else to do, I turned to him. "I love you Kyle," I said before getting out of the car and shutting the door behind me.

Afterwards, I couldn't believe it. I kept thinking it would get better, or that he'd call me, or that we'd run into each other and realize we'd been so wrong and we should be together no matter what. But that phone call never came.

Neither of us knew what would happen next. We hadn't considered the fact that we still lived in the same town, or that all our friends were the same. Our lives were inextricably linked, and we didn't have a plan for what life would look like apart.

the end of the end

A few days later, my roommates and I were throwing a party in the house we'd rented for the summer. We got several kegs and cheap clear bottles of vodka. We cleaned up the house a bit and invited our friends over. Before we knew it, our house was packed. My heart aching worse than ever, I drank my beer as fast as I could stomach, returning to the keg to fill up my red cup regularly. I was just topping off my beer when I spotted a familiar face near the door.

Kyle had just walked in.

I felt like I'd swallowed my heart. Somehow it was up in my throat and in the bottom of my shoes at the same time. Butterflies were slamming into the sides of my stomach like bumper cars and my tear ducts were stinging. I took a deep breath, steadied myself, and headed his way. I was hoping he'd want to talk. Maybe this was the moment we'd fix it.

"Want to go upstairs for a few minutes?" I asked him tentatively. He agreed and so we walked up to my bedroom. I sat on the edge of my bed while he stood, awkward in a room he was sleeping in just a few days before.

I waited for him to apologize, to tell me he'd been wrong. But when he didn't, I plunged ahead and did it for both of us. "I'm sorry. We shouldn't have broken up. I don't want to be without you. I love you, and no matter what we're going through, I want to do it together!" I said, my words spilling out in a jumble.

But he didn't feel the same way.

"Stephanie, I think this is right. I'm not saying this doesn't hurt; it absolutely does. But I still think it's the right thing to do." My heart beat faster, and my eyes flashed. His words tackled me like a linebacker, pain searing through all my limbs. I didn't know what else to do, so with my body full of beer, I got angry.

"Fine!" I said, jumping up from my bed. "Fine, if that's how you want to do this, then let's do this." I raced around my room, grabbing everything I could find that was his. My arms full of the remnants of our life together, I raced down the stairs with him on my heels. I pushed open the front door and shoved his things into his chest.

"Get out of my house," I snarled, and I slammed the door behind him.

Before tears could fall, I ran back up to my room, barely making it to my bed before I collapsed in a heap.

I didn't care that my house was filled with friends and I was missing the party downstairs. I couldn't see, couldn't breathe, the pain in my heart was enveloping the rest of me with cancerous speed. In my head I knew I'd survive this. But none of the rest of me was convinced. With no other option, I looked up at the ceiling:

"God…I'm out of ideas. You have to take over from here."

when life is cracked open

I don't know if you've ever reached a place like this—the place where your whole life seems to have fallen apart. Maybe it was your doing, or something someone did to you. Maybe you went through a breakup like I did, or got rejected from a school you'd been dreaming about for years. Maybe you lost a family member or a friend or a job or your health. Or maybe all of the things you were hoping would make you happy finally cracked and fell apart.

It's these moments when even the best laid plans fall to pieces—when we realize that no matter how far in advance we plan or how tightly we try to control over our lives, we may not get to where we thought we were going.

It's humbling more than anything else. These moments remind us just how small we are, just how little we're able to do on our own. They break the "can-do" attitude in each of us, reminding us that life is much bigger and more unpredictable than we like to believe. These are the moments in our lives that stand out like towers, markers of where it all fell apart.

But if we let them, these excruciating endings can mark the beginning of something new. When life cracks us open, breaking our hearts, our determination, and our hope, that's the moment we finally ask for help, hoping there's something better, bigger, and stronger out there that can rush in and save the day. And it's between these cracks—in our chest, our hope, our plans—when that something better can heal places we didn't realize needed healing and begin a rebuilding process more beautiful than we'd ever dared to imagine.

But of course, we are rarely able to see that in the moment. The next morning, my best friend Michelle called. I hadn't broken the news to her yet. She always loved Kyle, but she also always seemed to know when something was wrong.

"What happened?" she asked immediately. The grief in my voice was hard to miss.

As I opened my mouth to explain—the break up, the finality of it all, the shocking ache in my chest—I found myself without words. I took a deep breath and tried again. Again nothing came out. And then finally, a sob, "We broke up!" I choked out.

She waited a moment, a beat, and said one final sentence before hanging up the phone.

"I'm coming over."

She showed up 15 minutes later looking comfortingly serious. She knew exactly what this meant. She knew this wasn't going to be an easy one to fix. She sat down on my bed and I crawled back in. Then, thinking better of her position she scooted up and crawled in next to me.

"Alright, what happened?"

Chapter 3: Christianity Is for Grandmas & Girls With Ugly Shoes

Michelle has been my best friend for as long as I can remember. We met when we were 8, both much too tall for our age, and sporting straight-across bangs and braces. We met in a creative writing camp over fall break one year, and somehow as we sipped juice boxes and wrote fairy tales in little paper booklets, we caught each other's eye. 18 years later, she's still my very best friend.

We joke that we've learned everything we know about relationships from each other, but it's remarkably true. Michelle and I have been through every season of our lives together and know everything about each other: the beautiful things and the ugly things, and many of both. We've had ample opportunities to throw in the towel on our friendship, but neither of us ever have. Instead, we learned how to talk through conflicts and fight for each other when we'd rather give up. We've been by each other's sides for our entire lives, and no one in the world has had such a strong influence on who I've become.

Growing up, Michelle was my token atheist friend. She was

not raised in the church, and never affiliated herself with religion at all. In fact, during a particularly hard year in high school, our other best friend, Amanda, showed up at her house with a Bible. I thought Michelle might smack her with it. She *clearly* didn't think Jesus was the answer.

So when Michelle joined a Christian sorority and started going to a student ministry, the Annex, on Tuesday nights, I was understandably confused. But it must have been working, I reasoned, because Michelle seemed happier and more confident than I'd ever seen her. I'd watched her go down thousands of paths looking for her identity and self-worth, and she seemed to have actually found it. I was not about to question it.

I was proud of her, and I was happy she was so happy. But her faith existed in a different section of her life from me, and that was fine. I didn't dislike Christians. We just seemed to have nothing in common.

good product, bad marketing.

They say a customer is sold when they can see themselves with a product. Salesmen know the customer is going to buy the car as soon as they start picturing themselves in it—*the kids will sit here, my purse can rest here, my iPod will plug in there.* It's the same with a home. *This kitchen is perfect for entertaining, and oh the parties we'll have on this back porch.* Marketers know this too; they know unless you can picture their product in your life, you're gone and so are they—swept away in the flood of information, products, and offers we receive each day.

I'd never wanted to be a Christian, but it wasn't the doctrine that turned me away. Jesus had always seemed like a pretty good guy. To me, it was all about marketing.

It wasn't that it was a bad product. I passed by it several times on the shelf, nodding at it respectfully. But I just couldn't picture myself in it. There wasn't a place that would fit me. Christianity was a product geared toward grandparents and girls with ugly shoes. I wasn't its target market. I couldn't picture Jesus in my life, or myself as a part of His. And for me, that was ok.

For a few years as a kid, I attended a small Episcopal church a few towns over. Every Sunday morning we were dragged from our beds, forced to put on our Sunday best, and schlepped the 25 minutes to church. Once we arrived, it was like a senior citizen workout class: Stand, sit, kneel, sit, stand, sit, kneel, sit, walk to the front of the church, drink enough wine to feel it go all the way down into your empty stomach, carbo-load on communion wafers, walk back to your seat, and repeat the following Sunday.

But it wasn't as bad as some ex-church kids remember. I *liked* church. It gave me a sense of superiority for the rest of the week. I'd always had a fascination with being an "upright family." With the majority of my mother's family toting Ivy League bragging rights, and my mom's swanky Washington D.C. upbringing, I fantasized about being the family of a senator, looking like I fell out of the pages of a Ralph Lauren ad, riding a horse, and going to my fancy Episcopal church every Sunday. I liked to call myself "socially Episcopalian."

But that was it. I couldn't have even told you why Jesus mattered so much. He was an addendum to Christianity, a side-story, I thought. I didn't realize the whole story centered on Him, that He was the turning point for the whole thing. All I knew was I was afraid to become a Christian.

I was afraid Christianity would change me. I was afraid of it sterilizing my life—taking away the grit and the passion and the beauty. I was afraid that, instead of adding sparklers and champagne to my life, it would add ugly shoes and turtleneck sweaters, giving me a permanent seat in a life of Friday night Bible studies and boring friends.

I went on a few church retreats growing up, and I liked them well enough. But despite my attendance, I remember approximately nothing about meeting or interacting with God. What I do remember is Alexandra.

She had long blonde hair that reached her butt, and she wore denim skirts and strange shoes that I never saw in any store at the mall. But worse than her style was her attitude. She was a goodie-two-shoes, or a goodie-ugly-shoes as I liked to think of her (Look, nobody ever said middle school girls were kind, or particularly creative). And she followed all the rules.

One night my friends and I sat up talking late after lights out. We were laughing, and I was in the middle of telling a story when Alexandra rudely interrupted. She sat up in her bed piously and gave us a stern mothering look. "It's time to turn the lights off girls," she chided us, even though she was younger than more than half the rebels in the room. And when we rolled our eyes, she gave us a piece of good old fashioned motherly wisdom. "Early to bed, early to rise, makes a person healthy, wealthy, and wise." We were 12. I was disgusted.

It was then and there that I knew I wanted a lot of things in life, and none of them was to be a church kid.

But that day in college, with Michelle snuggled in my bed and my heart in a thousand pieces, I had no pride or fight left in me. So when Michelle mentioned a sermon podcast from her church that she wanted me to hear, I couldn't say no. She thought it might help; she thought maybe I'd find Jesus to be the glue that could piece my heart back together. I was too tired to argue. So after she left, I lay in the fetal position on my bed, and surrounded by tissues, I began to listen.

eat, pray, love

I was trying to listen, I really was, but couldn't process what the pastor was saying. It sounded like the teacher in the Peanuts cartoons. *Wah waaa waah.* I heard the words he was saying, but I couldn't make them mean anything. I couldn't make the connection. I didn't understand how this sermon was supposed to help. So I turned it off, more convinced than ever that I was going to have to fix this on my own.

And that's when I met Elizabeth Gilbert.

Well, I didn't meet her exactly. In fact, I didn't meet her at all. Someone recommended her book, *Eat, Pray, Love* to me, and having nothing better to do with my newfound singleness than read, I picked it up the next day at the bookstore around the corner. I flipped to the first page and began to read, my interest picking up like an avalanche with every word.

She got me. This woman I'd never met understood me. Her words of heartbreak, of longing, of feeling lost and depressed and hopeless, were words straight out of my mind—words I was too broken to string together. I read it like a bible—deciding she was me, and I was her, and whatever she did to get herself out of this mess, I had to do too.

She went to Europe. She found healing in heaping plates of pasta and leisurely strolls down cobblestone streets. She found new life in old languages and pieces of herself in the beauty of centuries past. She had a relationship with a god, something I had never considered before. She did yoga and meditated and talked about her insides like it too was a wild place to explore. And for the first time in my whole life, I considered that maybe, just maybe, there might be more to this God thing than I'd thought.

But first, I needed to get out.

I needed a break from this city. I needed to get away from all of the memories that seemed forever engrained in the sidewalks where Kyle and I had walked and in the restaurants we'd closed, sitting, talking, and laughing, completely unaware that the lights were turning on and the staff was beginning to clean.

Every season, every taste, every street, every landmark reminded me of the person I loved with more of my heart than I ever knew was in there—the person who was now long gone.

sometimes you just need to get out

Sometimes in our lives, we just need to get out. We need to leave. We need to go somewhere new for a change of scenery and a new perspective. Pilgrimages have been a spiritual practice for years, people leaving home and exploring somewhere new.

As we embark on a journey, whether it's physical like hiking the Camino de Santiago, or geographical like traveling the world for a year, we're challenging our outsides to something new, and getting away from what we see out our window every day. We can change at home, certainly. But something profound happens inside us when we remove ourselves from what's familiar and safe and challenge ourselves to something bigger.

This is what I needed. This is what Elizabeth Gilbert did, and it's what I wanted to do too.

I had always planned on studying abroad, and the timing couldn't have been more perfect.

I packed my bags with ferocity and determination. Each addition to my bulging suitcases felt like a step in the right direction—a step toward happiness, toward figuring out who I was, toward freedom from the ache that had throbbed in my chest for months. I was off to Spain. I was determined to get my life back, to come back whole and new and free of the hurt I couldn't seem to shake. I needed something and I knew this was it.

Chapter 4: Heaven & Spain Might Be One & the Same

I meant to go on this journey alone, but as I boarded the airplane with Kelsey and Michelle, I was so thankful I didn't have to. Michelle and I had not planned to study abroad together, but each of us had chosen to go to Sevilla without the input of the other. And now that we were leaving, we were so glad we were doing it together. Kelsey hadn't planned on going with us either. She was Michelle's *other* best friend (which made me a bit unsure I was going to like her), and she'd settled on Sevilla on her own too.

We were jittery, having just said goodbye to our families, nervous about being gone for so long. Four months wasn't a quick trip; it was longer than any of us had ever been away from home. As we settled into our seats for the long flight, I looked down the row at my travel companions.

I had no idea I was sitting next to the women who would influence me more than almost anyone else in my life. Michelle, my best friend for as long as I could remember, and Kelsey, a soul mate I had just met. We were heading into an experience that would change us forever, and we didn't even know it.

a tiny place all my own

When we landed in Sevilla, I thought I had landed in a dream. The cobblestones were perfect, with horse-drawn carriages clip-clopping down them past baskets of pink flowers and sunny yellow buildings. The Spanish was slurred and the wine was *perfection*. I was feeling very smug about my pilgrimage location selection. This was the perfect place for my life to change.

After our brief orientation weekend we were picked up by our brand new Spanish families. It was like a lineup in gym class, each of us waiting to find out which family would be ours. The woman who came toward me was a stern but funny woman named Asunción. She laughed that she was going to need to purchase a crane to get my suitcases into her piso (apartment).

We dragged my gigantic purple suitcases (yes, 'suitcases,' plural) through the city, the wide American wheels tipping off the narrow Spanish sidewalk at every turn. She spoke in rapid-fire Spanish that I struggled to interpret. I smiled and nodded, trying to listen, while gazing up at the colorful buildings that shielded us from the warm Andalucían sun. When we arrived at her building, I found myself standing in the middle of a cobblestone plaza, complete with a beautiful old cathedral and a panadería wafting the smell of freshly baking bread through the balmy air. Asunción slipped a small key into a wrought iron gate and we began the long trudge up the stone stairs with my luggage dragging heavily behind.

When we finally clunked through the dense wooden door

of the piso, she yelled to her husband Antonio to greet me. A boisterous Spanish man rounded the corner, loud and ruddy and larger than life. In his wake were two slender girls about my age, María-Angeles and Beatríz—girls who would promptly become my sisters.

Antonio laughed at my excessive luggage, making wild hand motions and repeating Asunción's assessment that we should have bought a crane, before dragging them down the hall to my bedroom. He opened the door and revealed a tiny closet of a room, about the size of the laundry room at my parents' house. It held a tiny armoire, a small desk, an even smaller chair, and a twin-sized bed—fitted snugly with Winnie the Pooh sheets. They helped me with my bags and then left me alone to unpack.

I closed the door behind them, and flopped on the bed exhaling a deep breath I didn't realize I'd been holding. It was the first time in a long time I'd had a space of my own. I was a million miles from my sorority house. I wasn't crammed in with other girls, didn't have to smile as they went to hang out with the group of Kyle's friends I was no longer invited to be a part of. I didn't have to worry what they thought of me, or make sure I wasn't left behind.

The closet already felt like home. It was a tiny space that was all mine—a place of my very own. I buried my face in the Winnie the Pooh comforter and realized I was free. This space didn't know anything about the heartbreak of home. It wasn't full of hurt feelings or grief. This space was new, fresh, a blank page ready to be filled in with memories, moments, and the stories of a new life.

red wine and best friends
(a few of life's greatest gifts)

In no time, Kelsey, Michelle, and I slid into a wonderful routine. We would wake up early and walk to class together, stopping at a small café on our way for tostadas con marmelada and café con leche (wonderful, thick toast with jelly and decadent, milky coffee). We'd sit in our classes for the next few hours—learning about journalism, Spain's history, and women's rights around the world, entirely in Spanish.

When our classes finished, we'd walk to lunch. We'd wind our way through the complicated Sevillian maze of streets and find our little restaurant—a charming place with a courtyard and delicious caprese sandwiches with queso fresco. We'd sip tiny cups of beer or thin glasses of sangría, and then head home for our mid-day siesta. At night we'd go for tapas on one of the famous streets scattered throughout the city.

My favorite thing about Sevilla is that it didn't require a guide book. There were a few tourist attractions and a museum or two, but it wasn't Paris. You didn't land at Charles de Gaulle with a long list of attractions that you must see to do it right. Sevilla was a simple city, and the culture was its star. The food, and the people, the dancing and the music took center stage. The Andalucían olives were the Mona Lisa, and the orange trees lining the cobblestone streets felt as sacred to me as Notre Dame.

When it came to tapas, it wasn't hard to figure out the best places to go. Tapas bars are famous for having no room to sit and for the locals who spill into the street, talking and eating and drinking late into the night. The more locals pouring from the restaurant, the better the restaurant. It was scientific.

On most nights, we'd join them. We'd order vino tinto (red wine) and sip out of gigantic glasses as we popped olive after olive into our mouths. The food was exquisite, the conversation was even better, and after no time we started to feel like locals, knowing where to go when and exactly what to order.

And those were just our week nights.

Almost every weekend we traveled to a new city in Europe. We took in the sights and sounds of the cities we visited, and made sure to check off all the cultural must-sees that had sat on our bucket lists for so long. We were diligent tourists, taking tours and hearing the stories and learning the history. We loved it. But intermittently throughout the day, we'd stop for my favorite part of each city we visited—the food. When I remember our time in Europe, that's what I remember more than anything else: the flavors, the tastes, and the conversations that happened around the table.

At night we'd go out on the town—savoring the local beer and wine like we did the cuisine, and laughing so much we cried.

I marveled at Kelsey and Michelle. They were loud and hysterical and would shriek with laughter without a shred of embarrassment when people looked over in surprise. There was something different about them, something I'd never experienced in my friendships back at school. Even though

I'd known Michelle for most of our lives, our friendship grew deeper by the day. This was the kind of friendship I was missing in my sorority house. This was the kind of friendship that exploded with color and life and spilled out onto the floor.

Kelsey and Michelle were kind and funny and confident in a way I'd never seen before. They seemed to fit in their own skin perfectly, knowing who they were and what they were about in a way that made you feel like maybe you could feel that way someday too.

And they loved me. Oh, how they loved me. All of the insecurity I had felt in my sorority house that last year, the feeling of being left out, or not measuring up, the loneliness I had felt was now gone. And in its place was a kind of friendship I didn't even have a category for. It was the kind that fills your heart up like a balloon to the point where it feels like it could pop. The kind where unconditional love is the norm, depth is expected, and fun is non-negotiable.

It was a perfect combination of seeing the most beautiful things in the world, eating the best food we could find, and having the most fun with the best friends any of us had ever known.

And at the end of long weekends, or as I'd tiptoe into my dark apartment at the end of an evening, I'd retreat to my Winnie the Pooh closet where I felt so entirely safe. I could be myself in that tiny room, and for the first time in as long as I could remember, being myself was good enough. I'd wiggle out of my clothes from the day and into something cozy. Then with my iPod speakers filling the room with soothing music, I'd slip in between the sheets with a notebook, slowly unpacking the hurt and the memories that were jammed into my heart from the last year.

Curled up in that bed, I journaled through my broken heart. That room felt like rehab. It was a safe space where I could process, where I could cry, where I could read and write and dream. And it was in that space that I began to pray.

I knew I was missing something. *Eat, Pray, Love* had shown me that. Something about the travel and the catastrophic changes I'd just survived had opened up a space—a tiny crack that began to grow hungry for something I had never wanted before. I was getting the feeling that there might be more to this whole God thing than ugly shoes and rule following. The god Elizabeth Gilbert talked about had nothing to do with cheesy Bible studies or turtlenecks. It was not the brand of religion I'd seen in high school and in college—vanilla and home schooled and lacking the champagne and sparkle I so wanted for my life.

I've met Christians who are shocked at the way *Eat, Pray, Love* affected my life. Her religious experience isn't Christian at all, rather Hindu, with touches of whatever doctrine or ideas resonated with her the most. But to me, the draw of *Eat, Pray, Love* wasn't religious or theologically specific. Instead, *Eat, Pray, Love* opened me up to the possibility that God was dynamic and adventurous and active in our lives, and that He didn't necessarily look like the people I'd associated with Him.

If that was truly the case, I wanted to know more.

Chapter 5: Yoga, Meditation, & Kevin Bacon

When Kelsey and Michelle and I arrived in Paris, I remembered enough about my summer in France a few years before and just enough French to help us navigate from the airport, onto the metro, and to our hotel—stopping only once to ask directions (the question in French, their answer in English, of course).

We made it to our hotel and lugged our suitcases up the skinny, carpeted staircase. We scrambled to find our oversized key, our hands full of way too much luggage for just one weekend. With a flourish we opened the door to our modest Parisian home and collapsed on our beds—a twin for each of us in a neat little row. The room didn't have much to boast other than a dorm-sized refrigerator, but the pièce de résistance was the balcony that overlooked Grands Boulevards. It was spectacular.

It had been a very long day, and so we resigned our travel-weary bodies to a night in while we planned our attack on the city the next day. We sat on our beds, curled up in our comfiest pajamas, making lists of everything we wanted to see and do:

Notre Dame, the Louvre, a picnic in front of the Eiffel Tower, and Sacré Coeur. But slowly, as our conversations always did, our discussion moved from the Champs-Élysées and Nutella crepes to something more profound.

I thought I wanted to find God while we were abroad, whatever that meant. But I didn't want to do it like them. While Kelsey and Michelle didn't wear ugly shoes or insist that we all go to bed early like middle school Alexandra did, I worried that their coolness was the exception to the rule. At the time, I didn't understand that what I was afraid of was a poorly cobbled together stereotype based on little-to-no interaction with Christians. I was judging a whole genre by one book cover in the same way Americans sometimes judge Parisians.

People pack their bags and head to Paris, convinced they're going to experience more romance and cobblestone beauty in their time there than ever before, but then they are often put off by a rude waiter at a restaurant or an unpleasant experience on the metro. "The French are rude," we say. Just like they complain that Americans are loud.

The truth is that *some* French people are rude, and that *some* Americans are loud. It's normal for us to take a piece of our experience and apply it to the whole. It doesn't mean it's correct; I know that now. But even though Kelsey and Michelle were lovely examples contradicting my preconceived notions, I wasn't taking any chances.

And so, with the picture of who I didn't want to be fresh in my mind, I'd come up with a different option of how I was going to find God. I was going to take a different route altogether. I wanted to find my God through yoga and meditation. Just like Elizabeth Gilbert found hers.

To me, yoga and meditation seemed clean, like the feeling you have after getting a massage or going to a spa. If Christianity had a scent, it would be boring vanilla. I was more interested in something eucalyptus-y and fresh. Yoga and meditation felt disconnected from daily life in the best way, otherworldly and peaceful. But the problem was that I didn't do either with any sort of training or regularity. Maybe my plan to "find God" wasn't the most thought-out, but it was better than becoming a Christian, and I told Kelsey and Michelle that.

Curled up on our single beds in Paris, I tried to say, in the nicest way possible, that I had a serious problem with Christians. Maybe I watched Footloose too many times and was siding with Kevin Bacon, but I wanted to dance! I felt like Christians had as much going for them as a plain sheet of drywall. I just wasn't interested.

So there in Paris, I took my shot, telling Kelsey and Michelle these concerns. I also told them about my Elizabeth Gilbert-yoga-mediation plan for finding God. I didn't have any problem with God, I explained, as long as His and my relationship looked like I wanted it to—specifically, sans vanilla.

Their reactions to my assertions, and to my yoga-meditation-God plan, spoke volumes about who those women are. To say they were understanding and graceful with me is even putting it mildly, especially considering I'd just compared them, their friends, and their entire belief system to a sheet of drywall.

With my opinions out on the table, and in the interest of research, I figured now was as good a time as any to ask them some questions. It might be good to know a bit more about the religion I was so vehemently rejecting, I reasoned.

the gospel according to kelsey & michelle (featuring stephanie as the peanut gallery)

"Alright," I began, adjusting the pillow behind my back, "The thing that bugs me the most about the idea of being a Christian is that it just feels so exclusive. I would think there are as many ways to access God as there are people who want to talk to Him. Does it really matter how? Can't everyone be right?"

"I know what you're saying, Steph," Michelle began. "The problem is that each religion has a different idea of how we connect to God, and what we have to do to make that happen. It's nice to say that everyone's ideas are good, but when you dig into what each religion believes, you find out they actually disagree; they totally contradict each other."

"But why does it matter?" I interjected, a bit more forcefully than I had intended. "Why can't some people believe in Jesus, and some people listen to Buddha, and some people follow whatever it is Mohammad said?"

Kelsey nodded and picked up where Michelle had left off. "Here's a good example. Did you know that the first five books of the Bible are the same as the beginning of the Jewish Torah?" I shook my head, confused as to how this related. "All of the guys you read about in the Old Testament of the Bible were Jewish. Christians and Jews share the same history."

"So why are they two separate religions?" I interrupted.

"Because, when Jesus showed up, the Jews divided based on who they believed Jesus to be. The people who are Jewish today believe Jesus was just another prophet, just like Moses and Elijah."

"Moses was the Prince of Egypt guy, right?"

She nodded.

"But Christians believe Jesus is the Son of God. The people who believe He is the Son of God are Christians, the people who don't believe that are still Jewish. They fundamentally disagree. He's either the Son of God or He's not."

"But why does that matter?" I said, frustrated that I still didn't understand. "Why does it matter who Jesus is? Can't Jews and Christians just agree to disagree? Why does it have to be this big thing?"

"Because," Michelle was talking now, "Christians believe that Jesus is the whole reason we're able to talk to God in the first place; He's our ticket into heaven.

"You know the story of Adam and Eve right? In the beginning, God made man and woman, Adam and Eve. They hung out in the Garden of Eden with God and everything was great.

Then, at some point the serpent showed up and convinced Eve that she should disobey God and eat the fruit God had told them not to touch. This was the first time people ever sinned, and because they sinned, they couldn't hang out with God in the garden anymore."

"Why?" I asked. "Couldn't God just forgive them? I mean, forgiveness is a part of love right?"

"It is," Kelsey chimed in. "God still loved them, after all, He created them. But they couldn't stay in the garden with Him. God is perfect, and they weren't perfect anymore. The two couldn't mix."

I must have had a blank stare on my face at this point, because she continued.

"In youth group when I was growing up, they used to do this illustration. They had a glass of clean water, and a glass of dirty water. The glass of clean water is God, perfect, you know. And the glass of dirty water symbolized Adam and Eve now that they weren't perfect anymore. If you mix even a little bit of the dirty water in with the clean water, the clean water isn't clean anymore. That's why Adam and Eve couldn't stay in the garden, because God was perfect, they weren't, and the two couldn't mix."

I still wasn't sure I understood why God was so easily tainted, but I let them continue. I could Google it later.

"So because people weren't perfect anymore, they were separated from God. Which meant they couldn't just talk to

Him when they needed something like they used to be able to do. The people had to have ambassadors to God, which were the priests. Because the priests weren't perfect either, they had to cleanse themselves of their imperfection before they could show up and talk to God."

"So how did they cleanse themselves?" I prompted, leaning back against the headboard.

"They had to kill an animal," Michelle responded, giggling at the shocked look on my face.

"That's disgusting! That's so tribal! The animal didn't do anything, why did it have to die?" I was trying to picture an ancient animal rights activist group.

"It's because the wage of sin was death," Kelsey responded. "Okay, that's hard to understand." She considered a moment before switching gears. "I want you to picture a scale. Got it? Good is on one side, bad is on the other, and when the scale is balanced, the priests could talk to God. Every time they would sin, the scale tipped toward the bad side, and in order to get back to even, they had to make a sacrifice."

"I'm not sure why the sacrifice had to be blood," Michelle interjected. We agreed we'd have to look that up later.

Kelsey continued, "So before the priests could go and talk to God, they had to sacrifice an animal and get back to even, and then they could talk to God on behalf of the people. But basically, this system didn't work. There were so many rules to abide by, and people were so terrible at it. It was like trying to climb a slippery hill. They were trying to do good things, follow the rules, be good enough, but they kept slipping. The rules didn't help them get closer to God, it just showed them how impossible it was to get there on their own."

"So that's where Jesus comes in," Michelle jumped in. "God sent Jesus to die on a cross as the ultimate sacrifice for everyone's sins."

"So we could stop killing so many animals?" I asked, shuddering at the thought. I wouldn't have the stomach for it.

"Yes," Michelle laughed. "That's why Jesus is referred to as the Lamb of God. He was the ultimate payment. No other payments had to be made after Him."

"And because of that," Kelsey piggybacked, "anyone can talk to God. When Jesus died on a cross, and when people accept Jesus as their Savior (which just means they're saying, 'I want what Jesus did on the cross to pay for my sins too'), that person is able to have a relationship with God. Jesus's sacrifice makes us perfect again, which also means we get to go to heaven. Jesus paid for our sin which connects us back to God today and allows us into heaven later."

"There are a million religions in the world," Michelle continued, connecting the conversation back to my original question, "and most of them involve trying to be perfect enough so you can be close to God. They all require doing enough, or being enough, or not doing that, or not drinking that anymore. They all involve what we can do, what we can offer, what we can become to be good enough to get close to God. But Christianity is the total opposite. We couldn't get close enough to God. We couldn't be smart enough, holy enough, good enough, brave enough, obedient enough to make ourselves worthy of being close to God. And so God came to us. He sent His Son to die so that all of His kiddos could be close to Him. God doesn't need us to be perfect to be close to Him. He did all the work for us. We just have to say yes."

We talked for a long time that day. They talked and I listened, then I talked and they listened, and when I asked questions, they answered them with patience and grace and non-churchy words, which I really appreciated.

But I still couldn't get there. I heard them; I understood what they were saying. But it was still on a cerebral level. It seemed like the message got caught in my ears and never traveled into my head or my heart or my soul.

I think this happens to us no matter where we are on the Christian continuum. Some of us have never been Christians before, and there are specific reasons we just can't seem to get on board. Some of us have been Christians forever, but there are certain things we don't understand about God that keep us from diving in fully.

We hear people talk about grace and mercy, we hear that our sins are forgiven and that we're free from any condemnation, but for some reason, we have a hard time living as though that's true. The words and ideas get stuck in our heads and never travel down to the places we need it, making God and Jesus and the Bible good principles and nice ideas, but never anything that changes us.

That day, I wasn't there yet. I still didn't quite get it. I still couldn't get over the way I saw it lived out.

Chapter 6: Not Fooling Anyone

The beautiful thing about studying abroad is that you don't study very much. During my semester in Spain, we were given ten days in April to do whatever we wanted. Three girls in Europe with ten days to ourselves—figuring out what to do with it was like sending kids into a candy store.

Within seconds we settled on Italy. Our reasoning was simple: Nine days of train rides through the Italian countryside, gelato, pasta, and carafe after carafe of delicious Italian wine. Yes. Done. Sold.

We arrived in Rome and within the hour we were seated at a table with a checkered tablecloth. Heaping plates of gnocchi, fettuccini, and spaghetti Bolognese dotted the small table. We poured rich red wine from the table's glass decanter and toasted each other, relaxing happily into our little Italian paradise.

The next day, we woke up bright and early, knowing that success in Italy requires a hefty amount of sight seeing, with frequent cappuccino breaks, of course.

We hailed a cab and headed straight for the Colosseum. We wandered around the ancient building, quiet with reverent awe. We stared at the walls, trying to absorb the depth of the history that had happened in that place—the triumphs and the pain that occurred on the ground beneath our feet. After asking the tour guide more questions than we realized we had and taking insensitive "let's pretend like we're fighting each other in the Colosseum" photos, we prepared to make the long trek to our next stop, the Roman Forum.

We exited the Colosseum to find a pair of silly and mildly charming British 20-something's, donning matching Pub Crawl T-shirts and mischievous grins. "Spanish Steps Pub Crawl?" they asked us, handing us a neon green flier. "All you can drink," they began, but they didn't need to finish. We got the details and promised we'd come.

wait a minute...do christians drink?

Before studying abroad with a few samples of the species, I was under the assumption that Christians didn't drink. It seemed to be one of those hot button topics, one of those cardinal sins that people like Alexandra wouldn't even think of committing. I thought alcohol and Christianity were oil and water—repelling each other absolutely, no buts about it.

And so I embarked on our study abroad adventure thinking I'd be the group's resident drunk, and hoping they wouldn't judge me for it. But Kelsey and Michelle's attitude toward alcohol surprised me completely, especially since Michelle and I hadn't broached the subject since she became a Christian.

Exploding my preconceived notions, I found out they loved a good cocktail. They demonstrated a relationship with alcohol that was about fun, taste, and community. They showed me a way to enjoy a good drink and a night on the town without the bad decisions, the blackouts, and the shame.

We would wander in and out of bars around Europe and have the best wine and beer of my life, but it was never about getting drunk. To them, alcohol was enjoyed the way food is enjoyed—savored, delighted in, a part of the cultural experience, just another thing on the table that people commune around.

We would sometimes drink too much, and sometimes not drink at all. But no matter how much or how little we drank, it wasn't the center of our universe like it had been back at school for me, and the motivation behind it was completely different. I realized that semester that drinking and the health of our relationship with alcohol has a lot to do with our own emotional health. I had learned the hard way the last semester that drinking when your heart is broken is like breaking the gates on the Hoover Dam—everything you were trying to keep back rushes forward and consumes you entirely. I'd seen alcohol as a means to an end. It was a way of drowning my sorrows, social lubrication, liquid courage, and a way of fitting in with people I didn't feel close to. In those ways, alcohol never gave me what I wanted.

But drinking with Kelsey and Michelle was fun and wholesome

somehow, and their ability to be free yet thoughtful with the way they drank alcohol blew my assumptions about Christians wide open. That simple action and the way they went about it showed me that Christianity isn't a list of do's and don'ts—it can be fun, silly and ridiculous and full of laughter. They showed me that Christianity can involve savoring good things, like wine in Italy and beer in Germany, and God's love doesn't disappear when you've had one too many.

And that was good news because that particular night, we did have a few too many, getting lost in a haze of loud Irishmen and limoncello and dimly lit cobblestone streets. I even came in a close second place in a beer chugging contest, barely missing my shot at the title. We were the happiest trio of college girls you could have ever found, wandering in a tipsy haze through one of the worlds most magical cities. We even got free T-shirts.

The next morning we peeled ourselves out of bed and set our sights on a cappuccino and Vatican City. Being the responsible and cultured women we are, we weren't going to let a late night interfere with our cultural agenda. So we put on our prizes from the night before, our matching pub-crawl T-shirts, and set off.

the sistine chapel

"Musei Vaticani" we told the cab driver in our most impressive Italian accents. As we wound through the honking traffic and zooming Vespas, we tried not to notice that we still smelled faintly of beer.

The driver dropped us off a few blocks from the entrance and we were instantly swept up in a crowd of camera-toting foreigners. American tour guides held up signs advertising their services, and we picked a nice looking girl, paid her our money, and ordered yet another cappuccino while we waited for the tour to begin.

On the tour, she whisked us into a world of paintings and God and stories. We listened, fascinated, as she pointed out pieces of art that other tour guides seemed to deem unimportant. But we listened with rapt attention, picturing the artists and popes and stories she described.

"As we walk into the Sistine Chapel," she explained to us while we waited in line near the entrance to the small room, "I want you to look up and notice something on the ceiling. Look in the very center at Adam and at God. God is reaching out to Adam, His arm fully extended, His muscles straining. Adam, on the other hand, looks like he's relaxing after a big meal. His arm is limp, and his finger is barely trying. If Adam just reached, he could touch God. But whether he does or not, God is still reaching for him. God will *always* be reaching for him."

With that, the door opened and the next wave was ushered in. We shuffled slowly, joining the throngs of international tourists that crowded the small chapel.

I looked up, quieted by the magnificence of the ceiling, and I caught myself wondering why Adam wouldn't just reach out his hand. *If God was reaching out to me,* I thought, *I'd definitely reach back.*

After fully taking in the ceiling, I turned around and caught sight of Michelangelo's fresco, *The Last Judgment*. I almost looked away, but then our eyes caught. I was staring straight into the eyes of Jesus, and my heart nearly jumped out of my chest.

Despite the severity of the captured moment, I'd never seen someone so comforting. Jesus's warm, brown eyes stared back at me, tugging at my heart in an invitation too deep for my ears to hear.

It felt like seeing a best friend after years apart. I was rooted in place, barely able to breathe, my heart pounding. But at the same time I felt like running over and throwing my arms around Him.

For the first time in my entire life, I was overwhelmed by an inexplicable desire to know Jesus and to be known by Him. *I just want Him to like me,* I thought fervently, and the inner critic who would have mocked a statement like that was suddenly quiet.

It was so sudden, so simple, and so profound—me staring up at this gigantic fresco with my mouth hanging open. I was speechless. Even my thoughts stopped in their tracks. There was no decision, no debate, no lingering questions or doubts or fears. All I could come up with to say was, "Jesus, I'm in." And despite the grandeur of the setting, those words fit, and so I repeated them over and over and over in my mind.

I had walked into the Vatican with a million questions. Why Christianity? Should I be a Buddhist instead? What about Hinduism? What is Hinduism exactly? But I left with absolute certainty.

I was in with Jesus, and I wasn't going to change my mind.

When our tour guide finally got our attention, we filed out of the chapel and into a courtyard. I pulled Kelsey and Michelle aside, and without being able to explain it any better, I told them, "Guys, I'm a Christian."

It didn't occur to me until later that I had met the Son of God while wearing a pub-crawl T-shirt and the slight aroma of stale beer.

what you need to know about god

That day told me everything I needed to know about the meaning of Christianity, and looking back even now, it still does. I didn't hunt God down that day. I hadn't begged Him to come close to me, and I certainly hadn't earned anything. I wasn't on my best behavior, wasn't wearing my Sunday finest. I wasn't even sure I'd brushed my teeth, if we're really being honest. But God didn't care about all that.

He didn't care what I'd done the night before or about the night of the David Guetta concert. He wasn't concerned with what I was wearing or even what I smelled like. He didn't make me jump through hoops, or become super boring first, or attend a certain number of Bible studies before He'd consider my application.

Instead, He came and hung out with me, where I was, how I was, on that day in the Sistine Chapel. He wanted to know me, wanted to love me, wanted to be friends with me, wanted me to get to know Him. And He didn't require a single thing of me for that to happen. That's the miracle of the gospel. God loves us, and He wants to be in our lives, and nothing we do or have done or even do in the future will change that. And it's all because of Jesus.

I forget this all the time now. I forget what happened that day. I still get caught up in the old habit of believing I can earn this myself, trying to do things perfectly, think good thoughts, act just right, and get all the answers correct, looking up at God and saying, "Ta da!" expecting Him to be proud and love me more.

And when I don't do things well, or I think stupid, selfish thoughts, or I'm mean or get all the answers wrong, I'm afraid to make eye contact with Him, because I'm afraid I've lost His love for good this time.

But whichever way I swing on a particular, messy day, I have to remind myself of what happened that day in the chapel. God came to me because He wanted a relationship with me. I wasn't perfect that day, and I'm not perfect today. I wasn't fooling anybody then, and He's still not fooled. But He still loves me. Isn't that crazy?

Chapter 7: Sex Tips

I was officially a Christian. God had been unwinding my fears about Christianity by showing me Kelsey and Michelle. The more I loved them and the more I laughed with them, the more I understood that being a Christian is a relationship, not a one-size-fits-all personality transplant.

He had surprised me too, teaching me little things about Him in the most beautiful places. I'd assumed God only hung out in prayer circles back home or with girls who weren't going to hold hands with their boyfriends until they got married. But there He was, in my glass of wine and at lunch with us in the sunny plaza between classes. He'd met me in the most beautiful cities in the world, making me wonder if a relationship with God wasn't one-size-fits-all either.

But now that one big decision was out of the way, I was immediately faced with another one.

I think most people who are in or considering a relationship with God have a few hot-button items that really rub them the wrong way. I know people who cannot conceive of the idea that God might be a Republican (I'm pretty sure He's not a registered voter either way), or that God would let bad things happen to good people (which is a really hard one to understand no matter who you are).

For me, I didn't really have a problem with any of the tenets of Christianity I'd come across so far, except for one: I couldn't possibly understand why Christians didn't have sex until they were married. But I knew that if I was going to be into this Christianity thing all the way, this was a detail I was going to have to wrestle through.

The thing is, nobody had ever told me I should wait until I was married to have sex. My parents told me I should be in love with the person. They told me I should be old enough and responsible enough to discuss and face the potential consequences of my actions. But nobody ever said, "Stephanie, you shouldn't have sex until you're married," and even if they did, I'm not sure I would have listened.

It's not that I was a floozy, I just didn't see anything wrong with having sex. Everyone around me was doing it, and if we're being honest, until Kyle and I broke up I fell to the conservative end of the bell curve, for which I figured I deserved a pat on the back.

But God had a different idea.

a hint of a promise

One week and two cities later, Kelsey bustled into the hotel room, a gigantic key clunking against the heavy wooden door, a victorious grin on her sticky face. She held it up like a trophy, thrusting her favorite pastry sky high for us all to see. "I found a meringue," she declared before taking another eggy bite. Michelle and I laughed as we rolled over, awakened from our travel-induced slumber.

Now on the third city on our Italian spring break tour, we were exhausted. But we also weren't done. We pulled ourselves out of our teeny single beds and began to search for the clothes we would wear to dinner on our first night in Venice. Michelle stopped rummaging in her suitcase long enough to sleepily wave her hand toward her laptop and asked Kelsey for some getting-ready music.

You'd be hard pressed to find bigger music fans than Kelsey and Michelle. They are always listening to new bands and going to shows. Michelle stopped inviting me to concerts a long time ago, right around the time that I wised up and realized "trucker" hats and mosh pits just weren't my scene. But they're not picky in their taste. In fact, while we were studying abroad, Michelle was convinced Lady Gaga's "Just Dance" was *her* song, and every time she heard it, it was God reminding her He loves her—a thought that warmed my heart to God even more.

Kelsey scampered over to Michelle's open laptop and selected a playlist to get ready to. Within seconds, a sweet melody was drifting from the laptop's speakers and I was pleased to hear we weren't going from 0-60, or from napping to Gaga. As I started listening to the words though, I turned to Kelsey and Michelle. It was a striking love song and I couldn't be sure if the singer, Phil Wickham, was singing about a girl or about God. You never knew with Kelsey and Michelle's eclectic taste. So I asked and found out the love song was indeed about God. *How was I supposed to know that?*

I kneeled down as I was listening to the song, getting close to the room's tiny mirror that leaned at the perfect height for a toddler. I carefully applied my mascara, still listening to the song's sweet lyrics.

"I rejoice in this divine romance, I lift my heart and my hands to show my love."

In an instant, I was transported somewhere else. Mind you, my body was still at the toddler mirror, still getting ready for our first Venetian dinner, but all of a sudden I could see something, clear as day in my mind's eye. I was standing at the end of an aisle, looking up at the biggest cross I'd ever seen, and I was really, really happy. I looked to my right and saw a man—not any of his features of course—but a man who loved me immensely. I looked back at the cross, knowing I was receiving the best gift of my entire life. And there, in my Venetian hotel room, something in my heart changed. There was a hint, a whisper of a promise from God.

"I have a better story for you."

And that's all it said.

maybe my plan wasn't the best

Compared to other people my age, my relationships weren't all that bad, but they also weren't all that good. Before dating Kyle, I was dating several guys at once, figuring if I had several of them in the queue it didn't matter when one (or all) of them disappointed me or broke my heart. I dated lots of guys, some good, some mean, and it hurt every single time one of them would exit my life.

After Kyle, things had gone from bad to worse. I dated more than ever, hoping that having a new guy in my life would fill the Kyle-shaped hole I couldn't seem to get rid of. But it didn't help. In fact, it made it worse. And with the recklenessnes that often comes with a broken heart, my standards dipped even lower, and my inhibitions sank with them. I wasn't sure where I'd fall on the floozy bell curve anymore, but I wasn't looking too good. But even that didn't help.

What I really wanted, when I allowed myself to hear my tenderest desires, was to be truly loved again. I wanted a good relationship. I wanted the kind of relationship I had with Kyle, one where I felt cherished and taken care of. I wanted a relationship with my best friend, with someone I loved being around and respected. But I hadn't been able to hold onto Kyle, and I was losing faith in my own ability to make a relationship work. So I figured I might as well hear God out, see what He had in mind for relationships.

sex on the beach

Three weeks later I sat on the beach in Palma de Mallorca, Spain. It was our second Spring Break, and we were traveled out. Having jet setted to a different country each weekend and spent ten days wandering around Italy, we opted for something a little more low key, in a tiny resort on the coast. It was the perfect place to rest. It was a beautiful resort with a pool that overlooked the ocean. They had a gigantic breakfast buffet with all-you-could-drink mimosas to begin the morning—just what the doctor ordered.

We'd wake up late and drift down to the dining room. Then, in front of huge bay windows overlooking the ocean, we'd sip our mimosas and talk. It was amazing that after so long we still had so much to say, but those days were filled with some of the best conversations of my life. That particular morning, the conversation centered on all things sex.

I was simultaneously fascinated and horrified at the Christian view of sex, and I was letting them know it at that very moment. "I just don't get it," I told them between sips from my champagne flute. "You're going to marry some guy without knowing how the sex is? What if it's terrible? You'd have no way of knowing!"

They nodded slowly—apparently having heard my argument before—and then firmly shook their heads. "It's more than that, Steph. We're not waiting until we're married because sex is bad, or because we don't want to 'test drive the car.' We just believe sex is something really special and we want to save it for someone who understands that. Have you ever had sex and just felt empty after it?"

I nodded slightly, not sure how much I wanted to give in to the point that was already hitting home.

"Well, can you imagine the next time you have sex, it's with someone who *really* loves you? And loves you enough that he just *married* you in front of all your family and friends? It's *that*. And when it comes to test driving the car, don't you think you'll know? If you're attracted to each other, you'll be able to figure out how to have sex. It's pretty basic, right?" They looked at me, knowing I'd know the answer to that.

Then, with no response from me, Michelle plunged on ahead. "There's a sermon series that our church did awhile back. I think you should listen to it. It goes through the book in the Bible, Song of Solomon, which is essentially a love poem with some pretty graphic sex scenes. It'll help you understand God's plan for sex and marriage. They'll explain it better than we ever could, and then we can talk about it more."

We trooped down to the beach, toting towels and beach bags and every English magazine we could find. We found a row of chairs under a colorful umbrella that looked over the expanse where the aqua water met the soft white sand. The beach was protected by jutting cliffs on either side, making a tranquil cove dotted with sunbathers and kids building sandcastles.

As I settled into my chair, I smoothed my towel out under me and breathed a deep sigh of relief. My soul always unwinds when I'm at the beach.

When her chair was situated, Kelsey pulled out her iPod and handed it to me all cued up. I took it, remembering the last time I'd tried to listen to a sermon—the week Kyle and I had broken up.

This time, as I listened to the pastor speak, I understood what he was saying perfectly. It was like I'd learned the language over the last several months. Not only that, the message didn't just sit in my ears, bouncing around like the story of Jesus when we were on our beds in Paris. This message went straight in my ears and hit my heart like a lightening bolt.

The message I was hearing as I watched the waves lapping the shore untangled everything I'd ever understood about love and rearranged it into something wholly different. The message was so beautiful; tears were now slipping down my sunscreeny cheeks. God had a better plan, and I was hearing it for the very first time. Relationships didn't have to look like I'd always thought they should. There was a better way to do it, one that hurt less and loved more.

His plan was better than waking up realizing the guy had slipped out of your room while you'd been asleep. Better than a relationship where you're not sure whether the guy prefers you or your body, and you're fairly certain you don't want to know the answer. His plan spoke directly to the hollow feeling I had always experienced surrounding sex, like I was naked in a way that reached far beyond my body and no reassurance could make me truly feel safe.

I had always tried to ignore the scared, unsafe feeling sex gave me, and I was never quite able to. But I plunged along anyway, because frankly, I never knew there was a different way to go about it. Not until now anyway.

But it wasn't just about sex. It was about relationships and marriage and love. It was a whisper of a love that stretched so far beyond anything I'd ever seen—the kind of love that makes you cry standing in its presence. It was the promise I'd seen while putting on mascara in Venice. God's plan. I'd wanted that kind of love for a long time. I just never knew it was possible, and I never knew what it would take to get there. But now I had an idea.

So halfway through the sermon series, I ripped the earbuds from my ears and leaned over to Kelsey and Michelle, relaxed and happy in their beachy daze. "I get it," I told them. They looked at me with surprise (I think they figured there would have been several more debates before I'd arrive at a place like that). But I was ready.

It rained heavily that night, so we cancelled our dinner plans, and ordered pizza into our hotel room instead. We ate and talked, a heaviness in the air as we knew what we were about to do.

After we were done eating, we climbed out onto our balcony, overlooking the ocean and protected from the rain that was now pouring from the sky. We sat in a circle and started to pray. With one on either side of me we held hands, and they prayed first. Then it was my turn. There on that balcony, in front of my best friends and the God I was just getting to know, I promised I wouldn't have sex again until I was married.

I didn't have to do this. I didn't have to make a sudden proclamation or make a ceremony out of it. I didn't even have to give up having sex for God to love me. But I had seen the hint of a different plan, and I wanted in on it.

I don't like the term "born-again virgin," because I totally didn't think of it that way. And I've never seen the phrase in the Bible, which makes me feel like it's churchy and weird. What happened to me that night wasn't churchy and weird—it was profound and beautiful and one of the best decisions I've ever made. I felt clean and excited immediately after we prayed, like I'd been given a clean slate. The possibilities were endless.

Back home, everyone around me had been having sex. It seemed like no big deal to me, and I couldn't understand why it would be arbitarily restricted for people who wanted to be friends with Jesus. But it also *was* a big deal to me, I just hadn't admitted that to myself. If I was honest with myself, I hated the exposed, unsafe feeling I got when it came to sex. I had just tried to ignore it.

I'd hoped there was a more love-filled way to have sex and that there was a more love-focused way to be in relationships. I'd wanted to believe relationships weren't just all about hooking up. But I had never seen anything like that before. When Michelle and Kelsey helped me see that God doesn't hate sex but that He just wanted to change the context in which we did it, I could actually see the wisdom there. It sounded like God's plan might actually be better than the one I'd been living. It usually is.

Chapter 8: A Million Miles from Emptiness

My Spanish mother, Asunción, woke me up early on a Saturday morning in late April. "Are you ready?" she asked me in hurried Spanish. I slowly lifted my head off my Winnie the Pooh pillow, trying to remember what she was talking about. She was out of my room as fast as she had come, shouting back down the hallway that we were leaving in five minutes.

Oh right, we're going shopping. I wiped the sleep from my eyes and my memory started to clear. The Feria de Abril was in a few weeks and I couldn't go in just any old dress. I needed a vestido de flamenco (a traditional flamenco dress), she insisted.

The Feria is a reason all its own to travel to Spain. It's the time when the city springs to life, and neighbors emerge from their winter hibernation to fully embrace spring. It's a weeklong celebration for the whole city. Businesses shut down, and people of all ages dress up, eat, drink, dance, and play together all day and all night. And so just like my mother and I searching for the perfect prom dress, Asunción and I wandered through the streets of Sevilla, in and out of shops stuffed to the brim with the frilliest dresses I had ever seen.

At first, I thought they were ugly. They were lime green and bright purple, blue and orange. They were mash-ups of fabrics and patterns and colors that clashed terribly. I finally found one that felt a little tamer than the rest and ruefully agreed to buy it, bringing a gigantic white and red polka dotted dress home in an equally gigantic shopping bag. I also had the earrings and the shawl and a huge flower that would perch right on top of my head. I still couldn't picture it, but she assured me I'd look perfect.

A few weeks later, the beginning of Feria had arrived. Kelsey and Michelle and I got ready together, Asunción, María-Angeles, and Beatriz pulling at my dress and tucking the flower in my hair. They nodded with satisfaction, telling me I looked entirely Spanish (never mind my blonde hair and light features). Asunción looked me up and down, her eyes settling on my feet where she spied a pair of flip-flops that had seen better days.

"Que haces!?" she screeched, insisting that my chanclas (flip-flops) were unacceptable footwear and sending me to my room for some more proper tacones (high heels). I obediently selected a pair of bright red heels and stuffed my flip flops into my purse. I'd change back into them later when she wasn't looking.

We took a taxi to the fairgrounds and got out blocks before the entrance. We joined the throng of people being corralled through the gates. We wandered the grounds, our eyes wide. It looked like a county fair with booths and games and food everywhere. But there were no fanny packs, no touristy cameras, and no Nascar T-shirts. Instead, all of the women were dressed elegantly in the shockingly bright flamenco dresses, their flowers perched regally on top of their dark, braided hair. The men were riding around on horses bareback with short black pants and even shorter black bolero jackets, and flat hats topping their heads. They looked exactly like I'd pictured Spanish caballeros to look. They were just as lovely as the women.

Then we wandered further into the fairgrounds and began to see rows and rows of large tents called casetas. It looked like a small town, each tent decorated differently, but equally as elaborately. Each caseta was filled with people talking and laughing and eating together. Loud flamenco music drifted from the tents, and pitchers of clear Rebujito (a fabulous mix of Sprite and sherry) donned each table.

Each caseta required a ticket, and we had invitations to two of them. We found my host parents' tent and presented our tickets. Asunción yanked me inside, showing her hija Americana off to all her friends. We laughed and drank from the tiny cups, speaking rapid fire Spanish that flowed more smoothly with each glass.

Then a handsome Spanish man came up to me and offered me his hand. He led me to the dance floor and we began the traditional Feria dance, Las Sevillanas. The dance was complicated and almost impossible to master. Kelsey and Michelle and I had taken a few classes and had spent hours practicing in Kelsey's tiny bedroom. But I still couldn't get through the whole thing without getting lost. Luckily, it didn't matter. We swung and stomped in time to the music, my smile reaching all the way up to my eyes. The man twirled me and spun me and expertly whipped me around, giving me the perfect time and space to throw up my hands in a theatrical, "Olé," clapping all the while. As we left the dance floor and I thanked him for the dance, María-Angeles hissed at me that I had been dancing with a well known torero (a bullfighter), Sevilla's very own celebrity.

The night had surpassed my every expectation. I gazed at the scene around me—the smiling faces, the colors and frills of the tent and the dresses. I felt the cool rebujito slide down my throat and a slight breeze tickle my warm face, and I was overwhelmed by the beautiful wonder of the life I was living. This moment felt a million miles away from the emptiness I'd left back home. I felt new and fresh and better than I had in years.

We began the trek home at 8 AM, having danced and laughed and played till dawn. The three of us held hands as we crossed the Puente de Triana, the iconic bridge in Sevilla, the Guadalquivir river glowing in the morning sun. I never, ever wanted to leave.

quiet healing

In the wake of Feria, I could barely keep my eyes open. Nobody goes to bed early in Sevilla, and after months of "When in Sevilla do as the Sevillanos do," I was desperate to catch up on some sleep.

I had been through so much since Kyle and I broke up, and

there were moments when I still felt the weight of it. I wanted to go home and leave as much of my heartbreak as I could somewhere over the Atlantic Ocean. If that was going to happen, I knew I had some things to work out. I'd been on a journey, a pilgrimage of sorts, exactly like I'd hoped. I had dropped old things, picked up new things, and I felt more full and confident than I ever had before. But I knew it was naïve of me to think some traveling was enough to heal what broke in the past year. If I was going to go home truly healed, I was going to have to face whatever was left. So that night, I turned in early to do just that.

I sat alone in my bedroom, snuggled up in my Winnie the Pooh comforter, scrawling words in my journal. I wanted it out—all of it. Anything that was left over in my heart, anything I'd left unsaid, anything I was still angry about, any unresolved fears—I wanted them out on the page where I could see them.

Once they were out, once I'd said everything I could think of to say, I began to pray. It was still unfamiliar to me, so my words came out in fits and spurts. But I plunged ahead anyway. I whispered to my empty room prayers for Kyle and for me and for both of our futures. I prayed for healing for my heart, the part of me that still stung whenever I thought about him. I paused for a moment, gathering up courage, and then before I could take it back, I prayed that God would help me get over him, something I'd refrained from ever saying to that point. Getting over him meant it was over, and I still didn't fully want that to be true. I didn't want to let go of him, but I wanted to *want* to let go of him. I had to let go if I ever wanted to heal and move forward.

As I spoke those words into my empty room, I began to cry, softly at first and then harder. As I cried, I remembered that night on my bed in Boulder, after I'd kicked him out of my house. I pictured myself lying there, the sounds of the party shaking the room around me. I could almost see my heartache through my shirt as I lay there curled up on my bed. The room felt cold and sickly, like a hospital room where death had paid a visit that night. I guess in many ways, it had.

It was the first time I'd really thought about that night since it happened. Usually, when the memory resurfaced, I would shove it away as fast as it had come. I wasn't ready to go there; I wasn't ready to think about what had happened or remember how the hurt had begun. But that night was different. I was ready to be brave. So I welcomed the memories in like guests at a funeral, sad that we were all there but welcome nonetheless.

As I remembered, I could picture myself in my mind's eye. I looked so small, lying there in that big room. My mascara had left streaks down my face like dry, black riverbeds, and I was clutching my chest, my heart aching in a way that was so physical it was surprising. I saw myself sleeping fitfully, tossing and turning like I was trying to escape my body, trying to get away from the source of the ache. My slightly older Spanish self cried as I looked at my younger self in so much pain. I wished I could put my arms around her or stroke her hair to help her sleep. I wished I could tell her that in a few short months she'd start to feel better—that things really would be okay. I felt a scar searing in my Spanish self, a reminder that I wasn't done with this. I wasn't free yet. Not completely.

I don't know what made me do what I did next. It definitely wasn't habit, because this was still very new to me. But all of a sudden, Jesus seemed to be the only one who could really help the poor little girl I was watching in that Boulder bedroom. So I asked Him to come in. I begged Jesus to go in and comfort her, and as I prayed, I watched her relax. Her tossing and turning stopped, and for the first time, I could see she was sleeping peacefully.

Suddenly, I remembered something that had happened that night, something I'd forgotten all about. I remembered lying on my bed, feeling like I couldn't breathe with the weight of the pain, and then feeling a warm comfort around me, an unexpected ease that everything was going to be okay. He'd answered my prayer, long before I had really asked for it. So I asked Jesus to do the same for me there that night in Sevilla. I asked Him to heal the scar in my chest, to fix what had been broken, and to make me new.

And He did.

I will never forget that night, because it was the first time I saw God show up. He was listening to me, and He was responding when I asked Him to (and even when I didn't). My heart felt different after I prayed, and I knew He'd changed something. Maybe I'd hurt again, maybe I'd miss Kyle again or cry about what I lost. But I knew God had healed me, I was fixed, I was whole again. God showed up for me that night, just as He had seven months earlier.

"God, I'm out of ideas, you have to take over," I had told Him, and He did.

the truth about god

I'd learned a lot about God since I'd arrived in Spain.

I'd escaped to Spain wanting freedom from my broken heart.
I'd arrived with a hint, a tiny shred of hope that there might be
some better way to do life than how I'd been living. And in the
last four months, God had blown my expectations wide open.

First, I had begun to see that God was nowhere near as
boring as I'd always thought Him to be. I wasn't sure how
He'd gotten the reputation I'd always perceived, but if the
last four months had shown me anything, it was that God's
not a God of boring shoes and turtlenecks. He's a God of
cappuccinos and art, of cobblestones and the fresh scent of
oranges wafting through the air. He's a God of dancing with
a bullfighter and being adopted by a brand new family. A
God of best friends and weekends at the beach.

Every detail of the last four months had been exactly what I
needed, exactly what I never knew to ask for. And every lesson
I learned about God was taught in a language I understood—
the language of travel and beauty and delight for the senses.

In our very own language, a non-churchy, non-cheesy
language, God had shown me who He is. He'd shown me
He's not the kind of guy who expects perfection, who is only
willing to talk to us when we've been shined up and dressed in
our Sunday best. He's the kind of guy who pursues us, loving
us especially when we've done nothing to deserve it. He had
shown me what life looks like when I live it with Him, when

I invite Him into the big things and the little ones. He had shown me a different way to live, a different way to handle my relationships, and a better idea than the one I'd been running with.

He'd shown me He can heal me from the wounds I'd picked up along the way in my life; I didn't have to tote around the same old garbage I'd carried forever. I'd asked Him to, and He'd fixed my broken heart, not just on the surface, but deep down where I needed it the most. I didn't know God could do that, or maybe that He would.

Most of all, I had discovered that when I let God in, I could see what His idea for my life was all along. I saw that He has plans and surprises up His sleeve for me that are better than I could have ever imagined—that I wouldn't have believed, even if I had been told.

Chapter 9: Who the Hell Do You Think You Are?

On our last day in Sevilla, we took a walk to all our favorite places. We started off at the little café near our school for a café con leche and a tostada con marmelada. We savored every last bite, trying to figure out what made the combination so intoxicating and vowing to replicate it.

Next, we walked to our school and said goodbye to all our teachers. Then we walked around the town center, taking one last photo of the striking cathedral and the Giralda tower that stood to one side of it.

We ate ice cream in the Andalucían sunshine and watched the water glisten under the Puente de Triana. We breathed the scent of oranges in deep, one last time, and swore with everything in us that we'd be back.

Returning home brought with it a confusing mix of excitement and sadness. Leaving Sevilla felt like leaving a piece of my heart behind, separating myself from a place that now felt every bit like I belonged there. But I was excited to go home. I had changed so much, healed so much, learned so much. I felt confident in a way I'd never felt before, and I was eager to test out my new sea legs in my old world.

what i wished going home was like

I pictured my reentry back into real life the way I think we imagine our first day back at school with a dramatic new haircut.

I'd walk back into everyone's lives in slow motion, an invisible fan blowing my hair back, but not too much to mess it up. As I would approach, everyone would stop what they were doing. Pencils would fall, conversations would go silent, people would stare. "What's different about her?" they'd ask in a whisper, sensing this intangible yet mesmerizing shift in the person they once knew. I'd be a new person, entirely different from the one I used to be. I wouldn't be afraid of anything; insecurity would be a word I barely recognized anymore, and everyone around me would mold to the new me like perfectly fitting puzzle pieces, changing to fit my new shape.

This is not quite how it went.

Just like it was in high school with that new haircut, I walked in feeling confident and deeply mature, and basically nobody noticed. And just like in high school, those who did notice weren't impressed with the new me like I thought they'd be. No, not everyone called me a Jesus Freak, but a few people definitely did. I also heard the phrase "born again" used as a noun. That was my new name, "born again," and although I only heard it a handful of times, I'm guessing it was tossed around more times than I was in earshot to hear.

I explained all that had happened to my closest friends in the sorority, and they were kind and supportive as best as they could be. But nobody really understood, and the worst part was everyone treated me like nothing had changed at all.

I think that's how it happens when we go away and come back changed. We expect the world around us to be different, or at least to notice how different we are and treat us differently because of it. But instead, most people just carry on the way they were before, mildly interested in stories from your trip or an explanation of what happened to you. But even then, the world around you doesn't shift quite the way you expect it to.

I had no idea what to do with that. I tried to hold onto what I'd learned. I started going to church every week, and I prayed when I thought about it. But before I knew it, the excitement of becoming a Christian, and most of the meaning of it, had slipped away until I was hanging onto a few rules by a thread- -one of which was that I still wasn't having sex until I was married. But other than that, everything else slipped back to how it used to be.

My friends were still best friends with Kyle, and whenever we were out my eyes would scan the room—half terrified, half exhilerated at the thought of bumping into him. My friends, now all 21, were going out to the bars more than ever. Not wanting to be left home alone, which is exactly what would have happened, I decided I might as well go with them. We made the very most of our newly minted IDs, taking advantage of every activity the Boulder bars offered.

For most of that first semester we were going out five nights a week, and I was dragging myself to class so hungover I could barely concentrate. And as often as the memories of what had changed in me in Spain would pop up, I'd shove them back out of my mind just as quickly.

Every once in awhile, boys would spend the night with me, thinking something was going to happen once we got back to my house. And most of them left in the middle of the night when I finally had to put on the brakes and, as casually as possible, tell them I wasn't planning on having sex until I was married. At that point, most of them grabbed their coat and left.

The first Tuesday night of my senior year, I decided to give Michelle's student ministry, The Annex, a try. I didn't know a soul, and I wandered through the crowd, my eyes darting back and forth, trying to locate Michelle and Kelsey's familiar faces. I looked at the people around me milling in the lobby before the service began and was surprised to see that they looked fairly normal. There were some girls I recognized from other sororities and even some cute guys. I was shocked! I'd always thought Christian guys were pimply and socially awkward, and of course, wore ugly shoes. But I had to admit, at least among this group, my stereotype of Christians didn't fit.

I found Michelle and Kelsey, and we found seats toward the back, settling in to watch and listen. The music began and it was actually pretty good—way better than the music from church camp (the music I'm sure Alexandra *loved*). I didn't know any of the words, but I stared up at the screen trying to keep up. I looked around for a moment and saw everyone else singing, not needing the screens at all. *How did they know this song already? It's the first night!* I began to feel uneasy again: maybe I didn't belong here, maybe I didn't fit, maybe everything I'd thought about Christians had been dead on. I still did not want to be a part of the kind of Christianity I'd always pictured.

But then, as the music washed over me, my feeling of unease began to disappear. It was replaced by something I was not expecting: total overwhelming emotion. Tears stung my eyes and cascaded down my cheeks. They spilled over by the hundreds in a deep, guttural weep. It didn't make any sense to me why I was feeling this way; I couldn't find words to explain it. I wasn't scared or sad necessarily. It was more that I was overwhelmed by the holiness in the room. I couldn't believe so many people were gathered together to sing to the same God I'd met in Rome—the same God I'd prayed to from my bed in Boulder the last time I'd seen Kyle.

I wept twice a week for the entire semester: on Tuesday nights at the Annex and then again at church on Sunday. Sometimes I'd go hung over, and sometimes I'd go to the bars as soon as church let out. But I'd go, and I had to admit I loved it.

I came to expect the crying, shoving wads of tissues in my pockets before I left the house. The holiness I felt in church was the polar opposite of what I was experiencing at the bars each night—of feeling hung over and feeling misunderstood and empty all over again. Instead, it was like rolling in the snow and then jumping into a hot tub; church was a shock to the system. But my daily life was just as hard to take. I was squeezed in between halves of myself—the person I used to be and the person I wanted to become—and I was entirely conflicted about both.

As time passed, life got more difficult. I think that's always the case when our lives are split like that. The weather got progressively colder, and so did I, feeling more insecure, lost, and alone than ever before.

rock bottom round two

That December was eerily similar to the last one. The town was frozen over, the temperature could barely muscle itself up past zero, and my heart felt cold all over again. The warmth of Spain was a distant memory I would have given anything to get back. Then during finals week, as luck would have it, our heater froze. We were left to study under piles of blankets, holding mugs of tea just to keep our hands from freezing too.

I missed Spain and seeing Kelsey and Michelle every day. I'd see them every week or so, and it was like a life raft delivering me safely from one week to the next. But it wasn't like it used to be. Our safe little circle had so many more people in it, and we had to fight for time with just the three of us.

To make matters worse, I didn't feel like anyone else understood me. Struggling to simultaneously live in the church world and my old world just made me really bad at both. It increased my insecure feelings of being left out exponentially. Life felt just as cold on this side of Christianity as it had last winter, and it seemed like nothing had really changed. Spain was this happy blip of warmth in my life, but since then, it seemed like God had been silent. He wasn't making my life better or happier at all. In fact, it felt like He was making things worse.

On one particular Friday night (just like every other), my roommates and I got ready and headed to the bars, wrapping ourselves in skirts that didn't do anything to keep out the frigid cold. We slipped and slid up the hill in our teetery heels and arrived at The Goose, the same bar that began (and ended) the night of the David Guetta concert.

We headed straight to the bar and ordered our usual double whiskey Sprites (I know…I know). We huddled under a heater, talking to our friends and saying hi to our neighbors. Guys stopped by to talk for a few minutes, and one of our friends broke off every once in awhile to talk to one she noticed across the bar. It felt like a dance, a mating ritual of sorts—people gauging each other's interest and pairing off for the night. I'd done that dance for years but had made a decision that all but took me out of the game. None of the guys in that bar were excited to hear anything about waiting until marriage. So there I stood leaning up against the bar, my potent drink freezing my hand in the icy cold weather, a spectator in a place where my life used to happen.

I watched the dance. I watched my roommates dazzle and laugh, I watched the guys eye them and, like sharks, slowly move in for the kill. I tried to laugh and strike up converesations with the people around me; I tried to convince myself that this was what I wanted, that I fit, that this was what was normal. But it felt like I'd experienced something that had spoiled it for me. I knew too much. My world was the same, but I didn't belong in it anymore. I'm not sure I ever did.

The truth landed in my heart with a thud, and without consulting me first, tears sprung to my eyes. Refusing to cry in front of everyone, I grabbed my coat and said a quick goodbye to my roommates before slipping back down the hill back home.

when god screws up your life

By the time I got home, I wasn't crying. I was too mad to cry. I opened the door and stomped into the foyer, slamming it behind me with a crack. My eyes shot to the ceiling, and I hoped God could feel my fury all the way up there in Heaven. He had come in, barely invited, and completely ruined my life.

"God," I yelled, knowing no one was around to hear me, "who the hell do you think you are?"

He had betrayed me. He'd flipped my life upside down with the promise of making it better, but nothing around me looked better—not one little bit. My relationships were worse than ever, my insecurity felt like it was eating me alive, and this whole Christianity thing—this whole idea of having God by my side every step of the way—was not turning out anything like He said it would. He was nowhere to be found, and the life He'd shaken up was lying in shambles.

He should have known how hard it would be to come back from Spain. He should have been there with me, helping me, giving me some strength or comfort or support—something. But instead of helping me, He'd gone silent.

"God, I gave you everything, and you haven't given me anything back," I raged, stomping into my bedroom.

I collapsed on the floor, cold and tired and mad. I had also forgotten our heater was frozen. Just my luck. I turned the dial on my small space heater and, wrapping a blanket around my shoulders, scooched up close. With my journal on my lap, I began to scratch away furiously.

Where are you God? I need you! I'm all alone and this Christianity thing just isn't going well. I feel like I'm in a desert and I need some water. Please give me some water, God. I can't do this on my own anymore.

I was done. That was it. I wasn't strong enough to do this on my own. I wasn't dedicated enough; I didn't know enough. This was supposed to be a better life. It had made so much sense when I was in Spain. But back in Boulder, my faith fell flat. What I'd brought home from Spain wasn't enough to sustain me here in the cold. It wasn't enough to make up for all I'd lost: the social life I'd at least felt somewhat like I was part of, the relationships I might have been able to have, and the security I would have felt by living in one world instead of split between two.

I needed some water, some help from God. I wasn't going to make it otherwise. I couldn't be a Christian if life looked like this much longer.

I fell asleep there, in a heap in front of my heater, still dressed in my party clothes, right at the edge of giving up on God altogether.

Chapter 10: An Accidental Missionary

I packed my bags for Costa Rica with much the same attitude and ferocity with which I had packed my bag for Spain. *I need to get out of here*, I thought as I tossed a pair of shoes onto the pile. *I need a break, a change…something.* Another pair of shoes plopped onto the pile.

The difference this time was intentionality. I meant to go to Spain. I'd thought about it, planned for it, and packed for it with great care. This time was different. I hadn't thought about Costa Rica. I hadn't planned for it. Hell, I barely remembered making the decision to go. It would be my very first mission trip, and as I packed my bag, shooting in the dark for what one could possibly need on a mission trip, I wondered again how I'd gotten myself into this mess.

If we're being honest, it was all Michelle's fault. She was interning at the Annex, and had mentioned the fact that she *might* be leading a mission trip that coming winter. "You could come…" she threw in there somewhere, trying to sound casual about it. "Yea, sure," I remember saying, barely listening. I figured I liked people well enough, and I loved traveling. Costa Rica has beaches, right? So when registration opened up and Michelle was indeed leading a winter mission trip, I was compelled by the sense of obligation that only comes when you really, really love someone. So I signed up.

There was no intention behind it, no grand gesture. I wasn't trying to get closer to God, because when I signed up, I hadn't known how much I would need a spiritual refuge. I also wasn't really trying to be a good person, or even a good Christian for that matter. I didn't know mission trips were a thing good Christians did. I'd missed the time in my church upbringing where Spring Breaks were used for humanitarian purposes. For me, breaks from school had always been used for trips to the beach and loading up on margaritas. But there I was, packing a bag with who knows what, to do who knows what, in some place in Costa Rica I'd never heard of.

At least I'm being a good best friend. The thought consoled me.

i'm not cut out for mission trips

We arrived in Costa Rica on New Years Eve, 40 college students, some who knew each other and some who didn't. I was sticking as close to Michelle as possible, my one familiar face in the sea of strange new Christians.

We were met by a tall, bearded Canadian named Matt. He had dreads and his ear pierced, and it took about four seconds before girls in our group were giving him "the eye." We piled into a string of big, white vans and took off toward the missions base where we'd be staying.

Even at night, Costa Rica was this melancholy mix of beautiful and hopeless. The greenery was overwhelming, lush and full, but the poverty was equally as aparent. Huts made into small stores hid among the brush, lit by single lightbulbs in the oppresive darkness of the night. The streets became progressively more windy as we zoomed up into the mountains. I was gripping the handle above my seat and keeping my eyes firmly on the horizon. Either Matt was a terrible driver, or these roads were out of control. Either way, it was all I could do to keep my dinner down.

When we arrived, we found ourselves at an old mushroom farm they'd converted into a missions base. It was in the mountains overlooking the city of San Jose—gorgeous, hilly country, with the city cradled in the valley below. There were dorms, a long dining hall, and a small chapel that smelled earthy, like wet dirt.

It was late, and we wanted to see the fireworks over San Jose marking the New Year. So we hurried to our rooms, boys and girls separated, and chose our beds before rejoining the group.

The walls in the large room were lined with built-in bunk beds, three tiers high. Michelle and I were feeling ambitious, so with our sheets and pillows tucked under our arms, we climbed all the way to the top and staked our claim before climbing back down and heading outside.

When they said, "We're going to the top of the mountain so we have a good view of the fireworks over the valley," I thought, "Great. We're already so high up, we'll walk up the road a bit and have a great view. No big deal." I didn't grab a flashlight and didn't consider I might want some more durable footwear than my Old Navy flip-flops until we veered off the road and onto a steep path you could barely see. This was not a walk, this was a hike, and I was doing it in flip-flops in the dark. We waded through streams, circumvented fallen trees, and leapt over ditches. I was covered in mud from the knee down before we finally reached our destination.

Sweating from the climb and swatting at mosquitos, I finally let myself wonder what the *heck* I was doing here anyway. I took in the faces of the people around me and was fairly certain I knew none of their names, despite the ice breakers we'd done in the airport on our layover. I didn't know them, they didn't know me, and we probably had nothing in common. I wasn't the mission trip type. I didn't even like camping. The mushroom farm was a good six hours away from the nearest beach, and I was getting the feeling that "mission trip" and "vacation" weren't exactly synonymous.

My eyes landed on Michelle, talking to a group of girls a few yards away. I glared at her through the dark. *Why did I let her talk me into this? This is a terrible idea.*

Then, out of nowhere, there was a loud crack, and the sky lit up with color and light. Michelle walked over and grabbed my hand. And together, we crept toward the cliff, San Jose stretching out in front of us like a sparkling blanket. The sky exploded with fireworks in celebration as the clock struck midnight. A new year had begun.

I don't know if it was the sparkle of the fireworks or the

comfort of my best friend by my side, but I wondered—a tiny thought at first—if maybe God was going to do something in this new year, if maybe things were about to get better.

That night I lay in my bunk in that cold, strange room. The building creaked and groaned with the mountain winds, and I nearly shot out of bed when rain suddenly began pounding on the tin roof above our heads. As my heartbeat slowed, I thought about this experience. I had no category or context for what was about to happen. This was different, something new entirely, and most of me wanted to scrap the whole thing and go home.

But that tiny thought was growing—*maybe God's going to do something amazing in this new year, maybe there's a reason He brought me here to Costa Rica.* That thought soothed me just enough to help me fall asleep.

dear god, i'm not sure if you're real but...

Much too early the next morning, we were woken up by a harmonizing bell and slightly off-key rooster. They crowed and dinged together until we were all up, grumbling as we clambered from our warm beds into the morning chill. I rummaged through my suitcase, having no idea what was appropriate to wear for the day. But I settled on a pair of yoga pants, zipped up my North Face jacket, and headed for the dining hall to find some coffee.

I woke up with new determination. If I was going to be here for ten days, I wanted to make the most of it. *The people here could use some help,* I reasoned, *and while I'm here, why not be the one to help them?* I was ready to work, to serve. Someone hand me a shovel! (Or whatever you do on mission trips…I still wasn't sure). But instead of a shovel, I was handed a journal and a pen and told I had one hour to spend alone with God. *I'm sorry… come again?*

I took the journal from the staff member, staring down at it like I'd never seen a journal before, and found a seat in one of the pews in the cavernous chapel. It was damp in there, smelling earthy and rich—a far cry from any church I was used to back home. I opened the Bible I'd obediently retrieved from my room. I had brought it along as the packing list instructed, but since I'd only ever opened it once or twice, I wasn't exactly sure what I was supposed to do with it.

I folded back the stiff spine and began to flip through. The words were unfamiliar and hard to read. I had no idea where to start. And so, as quickly as I had opened the Bible, I closed it again, opening my journal instead.

I have no idea what I'm doing here, God, I penned between the faint lines. *I'm so skeptical of this whole thing. How do I even know you're real?*

With that confession out there, the words flowed a bit more freely. It was just like journaling, except this time I was talking to God. It was sort of like I'd done in Spain, I was just a bit rusty. It was the first, carved out, on-purpose time I'd ever spent with God, and although it got easier the more I wrote, it still felt strange. The bell rang an hour later, mercifully rescuing me from the cavernous room and from bumping around inside of it with a God I still didn't really know. Then finally, we got to work.

Work clothes on and tools packed in the back of the vans, we piled in and began the journey back down the mountain. The van slowed to a stop and parked on the curb of a small side street next to a Home Depot and a Wendy's. *There's a Home Depot and a Wendy's in San Jose?* I looked around confused. I thought we were supposed to be helping people who needed it. This looked like the shopping center down the road from my house.

But instead of up the hill, we walked down, following Matt the Canadian away from the shopping center. The further down we got, the worse our surroundings became. The sturdy box stores were replaced with cardboard boxes. Tin roofs leaked as they attempted to protect the inhabitants from the elements. All the makeshift windows had bars, and kids ran around and through our legs, their faces smudged with dirt and their clothes hanging on by a thread.

We followed wordlessly in a single-file line as we wound through the shantytown, Matt stopping every few houses to say hi to a friend or to drop off a small gift. When we reached the center of the town, we found ourselves on a large stretch of dirt, surrounded by the shabbiest houses of all. There was trash everywhere, and the town smelled faintly of sewage. We gathered in the center silently, too shocked to speak. None of us had ever seen anything like this before.

Quietly, Matt began to tell us about the people who lived here. "They're Nicaraguan squatters," he explained, gesturing to their poorly constructed shacks. "They've come here for a better life." As he said these words, we gazed around again, wondering what in the world a worse life could look like.

"Many of the people who live in this town are in Costa Rica illegally. The best comparison is people from Mexico who sneak into the United States. In fact, they're treated much the same. They're looked down upon; they're seen as an annoyance— as the ones causing problems. Many Nicaraguans are pushed to the fringe of society into neighborhoods like this one. And although this life is better than what they had in Nicaragua, it's still pretty bad."

"This town has serious drug, alcohol, and prostitution problems," Matt explained, "During the rainy season, the sewage from the mall that you saw comes pouring down the hill and floods the town." I looked at my feet, at the plot of dirt in the center of town. It was bad enough as it was, I couldn't imagine standing in a lake of sewage. "The kids have no place to play," Matt continued, "no place to be kids, so it's only a matter of time until they get into trouble."

We were there to create a gathering place for the community, an expansive cement slab in the center of town. The kids could play there, even in the rainy season, and the town would have a clean place to come together. *A cement slab*, I thought. *No problem*. I'd seen cement mixing trucks, it couldn't be that hard. I pictured myself standing next to the large spout, looking proud as I watched it work. But there was a twist. Concrete trucks were expensive. We'd be mixing and pouring concrete by hand. I took a deep breath and followed the group to the vans. This wasn't going to be as easy as I'd thought.

hard work & hard love

We got to work right away carrying deceivingly heavy bags of concrete down from the trucks and stabbing them open with the sharp tips of our shovels. We carted buckets of rock back and forth, mixing and stirring the concrete in groups of ten, everyone pitching in and then switching to let someone else have a turn. The sun was hot, and we had to drink as much water as our bladders could handle, otherwise we'd get woozy in the heat. Despite the protection of my work gloves, my hands blistered and then calloused over from the abuse of the shovel. My clothes were thick with dust, and we had to wear jeans to protect our legs from the cement that would burn our skin if it touched us.

It was grueling work, but somehow I didn't mind. Some of the town's residents had joined in, bringing their own shovels and putting our puny arms to shame with their strength and endurance. I liked working alongside them, liked practicing my Spanish with them and hearing their stories.

I liked the hard work, even though I was pretty sure my muscles would never stop hurting. The faces of the kids playing around our worksite kept me going. They needed a place to play, and they didn't have one. I wanted to make sure that had changed by the time I left.

When we weren't working on the concrete, we went into the town's church building ("building" is a loose term) and played with the kids. We put on puppet shows for them and made arts and crafts. We learned campy Bible songs in Spanish, including one about Jesus being a superhero that stuck in our heads like glue.

I'd never been particularly good with kids. I never knew what to do with them. I'd pat them on the head and talk to them like babies, unsure how much they could understand or what they could or could not do. Babysitting had always felt like a minefield to me. The kids can't touch this or do that. They definitely can't eat that, and you have to discipline them this exact way. Kids felt so fragile to me, like I was never able to crack the code.

But these kids were different altogether. They were rough and tumble and loving without distinction. All they wanted to do was play and snuggle and run around and be carried. I could do all those things, I realized, and so the kids loved me. When we stopped for lunch each day, we gathered in the church to eat our sack lunches. I ate my peanut butter and jelly with any number of kids curled up on my lap, and I always gave them at least half of what I'd brought.

If you'd have described our time in Costa Rica to me before I went, if you'd listed the activities out like a travel brochure or shown me a video of the life we'd lead down there, I certainly wouldn't have gone. It was not my scene—not my idea of a good time at all. I didn't like to be dirty, didn't know any of the people I'd traveled with (except for Michelle), wasn't good with kids, and didn't know a lick about construction.

But I surprised myself with how much fun I was having. I liked the people in my group. They were funny and kind and not weird like I thought they would be. Nobody was trying to impress each other, and nobody was trying to be cool. There was no underlying competition; everyone just wanted to be friends.

Our group was so varied. There were so many different personalities, interests, and backgrounds. I made a friend who was literally studying to be a rocket scientist, and I met guys who reminded me of my friends back at school—only kinder, and funnier, and cuter, if you can imagine. I met girls who were so different from me—quiet and shy and reserved in a way I rarely found in the people around me. But I liked them so much, tuning into what they had to say, because when they did speak up, they said the most beautiful things.

I found friends who were like me, soul mates I couldn't believe I hadn't met before. They were sassy, funny, goofy, and interesting. I'd known them only a few days, but it felt like a lifetime already, like more Michelles than I even knew existed in the world.

I laughed more in those ten days than I had in years. The people around me were so funny, so creative, so quirky. Even packing our lunches in the morning was fun. I didn't know you could have this much fun and not be drinking—it was genuinely surprising to me.

The group's economy was different as well. People weren't judged by the same standards I'd gotten used to at home. It wasn't about what you were wearing, who you knew, or who liked you. I was grateful for a different economy, because I felt naked in my mission trip clothes. I had no makeup or cute outfits or any way to remove the cement from under my fingernails. I felt deeply exposed, but people didn't seem to mind. Because even though I looked far from my best, people still talked to me. They still asked me questions and wanted to get to know me. They wanted to know where I came from and what my story was. The conversations we had over cement at the worksite were deeper than the conversations I'd ever had with my closest friends back home.

I wished I had an ounce of makeup or something to make me look better, but even without it I felt more seen than I ever had before. I felt like my heart was on display instead of what I looked like, and to my total shock, people seemed to like what they saw. I felt nothing like the self I had gotten used to over the past few years, but I had also never felt so beautiful.

While we mixed and poured concrete, over our conversations at dinner, and in my quiet times with God in the morning, I felt like I was making a new friend—I was getting to know parts of myself and finding out I actually really liked the person buried inside of me.

Chapter 11: All the Way In

It was our last day in Costa Rica, and we were packed tightly into the chapel. We were quiet, the finality of the week like a blanket around our shoulders, drawing us in tight. The head missionary spoke to us, giving us the kind of pep talk that seems like it's incomplete without a butt slap and a "go team" at the end of it. And as he talked, I thought.

I thought about God and how I wanted Jesus to be my best friend so badly in the Sistine Chapel that day. I thought about the conversations I'd had with Kelsey and Michelle in those following months, learning about God and who He is and how He teaches us to live our lives. I remembered the night on the floor of my bedroom, praying my angry, hopeless prayer to God for help. I remembered how abandoned I'd felt, how I felt like He'd made things worse instead of better, like He hadn't helped me at all. And then, for the first time, I wondered if maybe I'd given up too soon.

I thought about my prayer the week Kyle and I had broken up—how I'd given up and asked God to take over from there. For the first time I looked at the full story, or as much as I knew of it. He hadn't fixed everything right away—He hadn't snapped His fingers and made my heart stop hurting, but He'd done something better. I thought about Spain, about all He'd taught me and how much had changed. I never would have thought about getting to know God if it wasn't for that broken heart, and I'd never have been able to get over it without God helping me through it and then healing me.

I wasn't certain quite yet, but maybe God hadn't dropped the ball when I'd gotten back to Boulder. Maybe we were going somewhere bigger, somewhere better, and I just couldn't see the destination yet. Sometimes, I knew, we want to embark on a journey but are afraid to leave the safety of dry land. We set sail but stay tied to the dock, leaving us stuck halfway between one shore and the new life we want.

Maybe that's where I was—stuck to the dock because I wasn't fully ready to let go. Maybe that's why I'd never made it to the other side, to the "better" I thought God had given me a peek of when I was in Spain. Maybe I needed to let go completely before I could see what He was capable of doing in my life.

I thought about my life up until this point, about the plans I'd made, the map I'd drawn for where I wanted to go. I thought about the career I'd been working so hard toward, the fact that I wanted to be a journalist, nothing else. I wanted to tell important stories, stories that would change people's lives. But that was *my* plan. It always had been. I had never asked God what ideas He had for my life before.

With the pep talk over, worship began. Matt the Canadian was up front, playing the guitar and singing, and this time I knew the words. Shoulder to shoulder with people who had gone from strangers to friends to family in ten short days, I sang the words with brand new meaning this time. I wasn't just singing them, I actually meant them. I was ready to give up, to roll up my map and hand it over to God. I wanted to see what He could do with my life when I broke away from the dock. I wanted to see where He would take me.

So with Michelle and my new friends tucked around me, I put my hands into the air, palms open and sang: "I'll stand, with arms high and heart abandoned, in awe of the One who gave it all. I'll stand, my soul Lord to you surrendered. All I have is yours." And I really, and truly meant it.

baptism: not just for babies

We crowded out of our rooms for our last dinner of the trip. As we made our way to the dining hall, we noticed a large blow-up pool outside the back door in the driveway. We peered into it as we walked by. It was full of water and looked cold in the chilly mountain air.

At dinner, Matt the Canadian stood up and made an announcement. "We've gotten a few requests for baptisms tonight. So if this is something you might want to do, get into your bathing suit after dinner, and we'll all meet out back in the driveway."

"That's what the pool was for," we all murmured, understanding now.

I had never thought about being baptized before. I'd been sprinkled as a baby in a church I barely remembered going to, and I figured that counted well enough. Just then, Michelle slid up to me. I wasn't sure where she'd been during dinner. "Can I talk to you?" she asked breathlessly. She grabbed my arm and led me around a corner where we could talk privately.

"I want to get baptized," she confessed. "I've always wanted to, ever since I became a Christian, but I've never had the chance. I think tonight is the perfect time, and I really want to do it."

"You were never baptized as a baby?" I asked incredulously. If *I* had been, I thought everybody had. But she looked at me like I should have known better. "Do you know of *any* time I went to church before I came to college?" she asked, "because I certainly don't." She had a point.

"I think you should do it!" I encouraged. Then I paused, "I was baptized when I was little, so I guess that was my shot, right?"

"Not at all," she replied. "Lots of people are baptized when they're babies, but it's a totally different thing to decide to do it on your own. I have tons of friends who have been baptized recently. It's a really profound statement when it's your choice because it's a declaration of your faith, not just what your parents want."

"Um…would you want to do it with me?" she began hesitantly, letting the question trail off into the breeze. But I was nodding before she even asked. I did want to be baptized. I was sure of it. And I wanted to do it together.

Fully charged, we sprinted to our room and grabbed the one-pieces we'd brought to go to the beach on our one day off. We slipped them on and grabbed towels, sliding our feet into flip-flops and running back out to the driveway.

Everyone had gathered by the time we got back, and someone was playing worship music faintly in the background. Matt locked eyes with me and Michelle and nodded in our direction. He'd let us know when it was time. We sang and prayed, the 40 of us in a tight circle, united by this experience.

"Thank you God," Matt began praying out loud. "Thank you for sending your Son to die on the cross for us. Thank you that because of Him, we get to start over, we get a clean slate. Thank you that just like Jesus died and was raised from the dead, you give us that very same opportunity in baptism.

You give us the chance to declare in front of our friends and community that we want what Jesus did on the cross to count for us. We want our old life, the mess of it, the hurt of it, the brokenness of it to die, and to be given new life."

He motioned Michelle forward.

She stepped into the baby pool, the shock of the cold water evident on her face. Matt and another leader held her arms gently on either side as they prayed for her. Finally, when it was time, they said, "Michelle, we baptize you in the name of the Father, and of the Son, and of the Holy Spirit." And with that, in one smooth motion she bent her knees, they leaned her back, and dunked her entirely in the freezing cold water. Her head broke the surface of the water as she stood to cheers and whistles form the whole circle, minus me. I couldn't cheer. Happy, proud tears were pouring down my cheeks. I couldn't make a sound.

Michelle's life had always been proof to me that God existed. I knew her for years before she met Him, and it was impossible not to believe in God after seeing what He'd done in her life. She was still Michelle after becoming a Christian, but a truer version of herself. She was stronger, more confident, funnier, more authentically her. She fit in her skin, you could just tell, not rattling around trying to find where she belonged like most of us were doing.

Her baptism described it perfectly—when she became a Christian it really did seem like all the dead, hurting, broken parts of her were washed away, and what was left in their place was like nothing I'd ever seen before. She looked like her, like my best friend, the way she was always meant to be. I knew she couldn't have done that on her own. God had to be real.

I wanted Him to be that real in my life too. I needed a declaration, a once-and-for-all proclamation that I was breaking free of the shore I had been so afraid to leave. I wanted to cut the rope and sail off someplace new. I wanted to see what God was capable of. I wanted to dive in fully, giving Him my map and my best laid plans, and see what He could make of the life I'd been trying to make on my own for so long.

So then it was my turn.

I handed my towel to a now sopping wet Michelle and walked toward the baby pool. I gingerly stepped into the cold water, my heart pounding in my ears. Matt held my arm on one side, the other leader held it on the other, and they prayed for me—a sweet, gentle prayer. I had prayed for water, and God was giving it to me—more than I ever would have believed even if He had told me.

I took a deep breath, *God*, I said in my mind, *I'm in. All the way this time.*

And with that, they dunked me.

changed

The next evening, my parents picked me up from the airport in Denver. We were a ragged looking bunch, still in our missionary attire, our clothes caked with cement and dirt. "You guys look like you just got voted off the island," my dad laughed as I introduced him to all my new friends.

They drove me home and got me some food before ushering me up to bed for a good night's sleep before I headed back up to school. They insisted that I shower in between dinner and bed, something my dirty missionary self found *totally* unnecessary. I'd gotten used to the dirt. It didn't bother me anymore. But I conceded. Fed, clean, my hair freshly washed and brushed through, my clothes safely in the washing machine, I climbed into bed and took a long, deep breath.

So much had happened in the last ten days. It almost seemed like a lifetime had passed since I'd packed my bags just a week and a half before. The room I'd lived in since I was five looked unfamiliar, the white walls looked strange and stark in comparison to the uneven wood I'd run my fingers along while lying on my third tier bunk. I missed Michelle, her head touching mine, reaching back to hold hands when the creak of the room or the rain on the tin left us scared.

This time, I was alone.

My mind flipped through a slideshow of our time in Costa Rica. I could see the mushroom farm and smell the earthy chapel that at first felt so empty, but was so full and safe by the end. I could hear the giggles of the children I'd come to adore. I could almost feel their little hands in mine or hear them crunching through my bag of potato chips as they snuggled into my lap during lunch. I could feel the purpose and love I'd felt while working for people I didn't even know. I understood love in a new way somehow—my hands calloused and cut from the hard work we'd poured into that concrete.

It's amazing how much you love people when you end up bleeding for them, I thought. Or maybe it's the other way around: it's amazing how much you'll bleed for someone when you love them. I was surprised I could love people I'd never met before, but I loved the people in that tiny, broken town. I really did.

I could see the faces of my group—this strange little family

I'd never asked for or imagined. They were so different from who I thought they would be—true friends in a place I never expected to find them. I liked them so much, this group of Christians. I laughed at the thought, remembering how absurd I would have thought that was just a few weeks before. But I did. They showed me something I never expected: a group of people who really saw me, really cared about me, really sought to understand me. I fit with them. For the first time in as long as I could remember, I really fit.

I replayed that last day in my head—the safety I felt surrounded by my new friends, the swell I felt in my chest as I sang with my arms high up in the air. I could feel the rope breaking, the one that had held me to the dock for so long, but I didn't have to cut it alone. I was surrounded. I had friends who were going with me. And when my body hit the water in that baby pool, the rope snapped completely, and I emerged to uproarious applause.

I was homesick, even though I was home. I missed every person, every detail, every moment. It ached. I wanted to go back, wanted to do it again, wanted more. I'd only just gotten a taste.

It felt like falling asleep after a day in the ocean. You can feel the rocking of the waves long after you're on dry land. But I didn't want the rocking to stop. If it stopped, it meant it was over.

It scared me to feel this way. It felt like the all-too-familiar feeling of falling in love—this sort of intoxicating love that swallows you whole, and you can't be swallowed fast enough. It felt like an invisible hand was reaching out from the space between my ribs and grasping for something that I had for awhile, but all of a sudden couldn't find. There was something that I'd gotten used to in Costa Rica, some intangible something that made life explode with meaning. And there, closed in by the stark, lonely walls of my bedroom, I knew that whatever it was, I desperately wanted it back.

And then it hit me. The lightbulb went off, and I suddenly realized exactly what I had experienced in Costa Rica. That ache in my chest, that tumbling, out-of-control feeling of falling in love wasn't just for my new friends or the feeling of my gloves covered in hardening concrete. I wasn't just missing those kiddos or the mushroom farm with the creepy sounds that kept us up at night. What I'd experienced in Costa Rica—the intangible thing that my heart was reaching for—was God.

Chapter 12: Life Without a Map

This time, going back to school was altogether different. I didn't care what everyone thought. I was fundamentally different and didn't care if anyone noticed or approved. This time, I also wasn't alone. I'd had Michelle and Kelsey when I came home from Spain, but that was it. This time I had Michelle, Kelsey, and a whole slew of new friends who got me, and having a team like that backing you up can give you the courage to do anything.

It also wasn't a half-change this time. I wasn't living in the middle, trying to fit in one world and the other, seeing what I could get away with or how little I could do and still be alright. I was in completely this time, sailing toward a new way of doing things as fast as my little boat could take me.

The day after we got back, I started a new internship at a TV station. This was the pinicle of my journalism career so far—an internship I'd applied for three times before finally getting a spot. I had been so excited, telling people who didn't even ask what I'd be doing in the spring. But when I arrived the first day, something was drastically different.

I loved journalism; there was nothing like it for me. I had wanted to be a journalist for years, and usually could think of nothing else. But walking into the news room that first day, something was different. Journalism was the same, but I wasn't. My love for the profession was gone completely, almost overnight. I dragged my feet through that first day, wishing I could be back with my friends or doing something to change the hurting I saw going on in the world instead of editing videos in a cold, dark room.

I slipped my headphones into my iPod and played a sermon from my church I'd missed while we were in Costa Rica, working half-heartedly while wishing I could do something more.

i have to go back

Two days after we got back from Costa Rica, an earthquake destroyed Haiti. Our Costa Rica team watched in horror as news flooded in of a country in ruins. We watched children cry, parents search for loved ones, and bodies stack up. We cried together, seeing the faces of the Costa Ricans we so loved in the eyes of the hurting Haitians. We wanted to go, had to go, had to leave, had to go back. But we couldn't. Haiti couldn't support any relief teams yet, so I did the next best thing I could think of.

I knew what I had to do if I was going to be a journalist. I only had a few months left before I graduated and needed to find another internship for that coming summer. I knew what

I was supposed to do in life, what the next stop on my map should be, but I wanted something different. I wasn't holding the map anymore. God was, and I wanted to go where He wanted me to be.

So when I received an offer to live in Washington, D.C. for the summer to work for a TV station, I took a deep breath, turned it down, and signed up for another mission trip, to Ghana this time.

Every misconception I had about God and Christianity had been blown out of the water. God was thrilling and dangerous and safe all at the same time. He was wild. He would send you to the corners of the world if you said you were willing and would heal your wounds with soothing tenderness. He was everything good about life wrapped up into one. He was French wine and Spanish olives and Italian cappuccinos. He was quiet times in Costa Rica and being baptized in the mountains and best friends and the creakiest bunk beds. He was fireworks and adventure and love that seeped into every corner, spreading farther than the eye can see. And I wanted more of Him.

This wasn't normal; it wasn't what I was expected to do so close to graduation. But I was learning that when I did things God's way instead of mine, better things than I could have ever imagined would happen. And that's what I wanted. He was what I wanted. I didn't want normal or the plan I'd so carefully mapped out. I wanted something new, something better, and I knew exactly Who I needed to follow if I was going to get there.

ghana and the lipstick gospel

A few months later, I was off. For ten weeks, I'd be doing mission work in Ghana, West Africa. My bag was packed full of dry shampoo and bottles of bug spray. I even brought a large jar of peanut butter at one of my friend's urging. "Trust me, you'll want it," she coaxed comfortingly as she zipped up my suitcase.

When my small team and I arrived in Ghana, the airport looked reassuringly familiar. I had never been to Africa before, and didn't know what to expect. But this calm, clean airport was a good start; I began to relax. And then we stepped out of the front doors and into total chaos.

There were men, women, and children clawing at us, trying to carry our bags for a bit of spare change. Shouts and inquiries flooded our ears while curious eyes examined us on every side. Merchants, food vendors, and beggars peppered the mass of people that filled the lot outside the airport from edge to edge. We found our host quickly, and he ushered us into a hot car. Children and old men pounded at the windows, hands outstretched. White people mean money, we found out later. We avoided eye contact guiltily for a while before finally motioning sheepishly that we didn't have any money to give.

We drove out of the city and past more throngs of people. There were women in the middle of the road with baskets on their heads, selling everything from eggs to ice cream to pieces of goat meat. And when we finally arrived at the place where we would stay, I felt guilty for my relief when huge metal gates slammed closed tightly behind us.

We spent the next several days acclimating to the climate and the culture, and we ventured out of our compound several times to play soccer with the neighbor kids. Each day I woke up in Ghana I was more and more comfortable, my insides finally making peace with the frantic change of my surroundings.

Our ministry in Ghana was simple. We were preachers, brought into most remote villages to share the word of God. At first I was horrified at this prospect. When I pictured preachers and street evangelists, I pictured people with doomsday posters screaming at the "sinners" passing by. I pictured the people who knocked on stranger's doors, imposing their views on people who were just trying to enjoy their morning coffee. I had been a Christian for 30 seconds it felt like—I wasn't ready to have my own slot as a televangelist.

But as we arrived in various villages, I was surprised to see the throngs of people who came to hear us speak. I was even more surprised to watch as hundreds of people gave their lives to Jesus, devouring the message we brought. People asked us questions and asked us to pray for them, bringing babies and old women and placing them in front of us, wanting us to pray to God on their behalf.

The Bible came to life for me in those ten weeks. Jesus' parables about farming and sheep and goats all of a sudden made perfect sense in the primitive villages we visited. Each place we went a crowd always seemed to form, and I tried to imagine how Jesus felt—people always flocking around Him for help, bringing their sick and dying family members. Their trust was humbling, but inspiring. We prayed for babies and sick people and visited widows the town largely ignored. The Bible sprang to life for me that summer because I needed it. I needed its insight and wisdom and comfort in ways I never had before.

I'd always felt like the Bible was a bit outdated, secretly thinking God should come out with an updated version with parables about iPhones or something. "Thou shalt not covet thy neighbor's well groomed eyebrows in her selfie." But being there in those villages, I got to see the universal truths the Bible contained and the universal experiences we have as people. Death happens everywhere, loss is universal. Joy and laughter and smiling are universal too, as is a need for God.

The people we met in those villages, young and old, needed the exact same things I needed—to know they were loved, not alone, to have help in their mess and comfort when they were hurting. I never knew we were so much the same, even when our lives, on the surface, looked so different.

We'd show up in villages, and sometimes I'd have to preach. I got to share stories and ideas and the passages from scripture I was pouring over each morning—it making sense for the very first time. I got to watch as my stories impacted the people listening to them. They'd hug me tightly, saying, "Thank you sista," when I was finished.

But the best part of each service was the worship. To me, worship had always meant fog machines and live bands in dark, air-conditioned churches. But what the Ghanaians taught us was worship on a whole other level. We'd get to a village and someone would grab a drum. Before we knew it, the whole village would be dancing in a circle, clapping in beautiful rhythms we couldn't mimic, despite our best efforts. The dancing was wild and the songs were joyful, some in accented English and the rest in any number of tribal languages they spoke in that region.

I danced and danced and held sticky little hands and snuggled the most beautiful babies, bouncing and giggling on my hip, fascinated with my blonde hair. The people in Ghana showed me a new kind of worship—one that happened organically, reaching up to the heavens beneath a sprinkling of stars.

god is anything but boring

Halfway through our trip, as we were visiting a village near our house, one of our favorite pastors came up to us with a handful of sticks. "Draw," he instructed us. As we each pulled a stick from his hand, I looked at mine, surprised to see it was the shortest one in the bunch. "Let's go!" he said to me, and he nodded toward his motorcycle. "We have some families to visit."

I stepped gingerly on the back of the bike, wrapping my arms around the massive man who had become an instant father figure to us. He gunned the motorcycle and we sped down a dirt road—a road that quickly became nothing more than a thin path and every so often disappeared into thick brush with no discernible way through.

A few times we had to get off of the bike and roll it through a small stream or up a big hill as we ventured deeper and deeper into the African bush. We were far away from anything familiar at that point—far away from cities and towns and venturing into the land somewhere near the Burkina Faso border.

I held on tightly as branches whipped at my legs. Their smacks stung, but my smile couldn't be erased—this was the most dangerous thing I'd ever done, certainly. There were all kinds of animals out there, anything could happen, and a little bit of rain could strand us there for days. But I'd never felt more alive. I grinned like a fool on the back of the motorcycle. My heart felt weightless as we evaded roots and carved around trees. As I laughed and squealed, my heart light with adventure, my thoughts began to drift back home.

I began thinking of my friends from my sorority and what they might be doing at that very moment. I pictured several of them lifeguarding at their neighborhood pools, postponing adult life just one summer longer in favor of cocktails and no tan lines. I knew I was missing out, that they would have memories and pictures and lives together that I wasn't a part of. But for the first time in my life, I just didn't care. I hadn't chosen the normal route. There was nothing normal about this route to be sure, but this fit me.

As we pulled into the remote village, we zoomed past a leopard's skin that had been stretched out to dry. I shook my head, opening my eyes wider, *A leopard skin? A real one?* We waved to a pair of old men resting in the shade on wooden benches, shocked to see a white girl zooming through their village. As I laughed and held on tightly, my heart squeezed in my chest. *God,* I thought, *this is why you're anything but boring,* my misconception about Christians shattered for good in the bright Ghanaian sun.

I was a new person on the back of that motorcycle. God had scrubbed away my broken bits, revealing a person who fit in her skin—the woman I was always meant to be.

now what?

That night, I laid in my bunk bed wide awake while the rest of my team was sleeping. Surrounded by an itchy blue mosquito net, I propped my legs up on the bottom of the bunk above me, trying not to scratch my mosquito bites and failing miserably. I pictured zooming through the bush on the motorcycle that day. In my mind's eye, I could see the smile plastered across my face, but there was one piece still missing.

I thought I knew what I wanted to do with my life—I had always been a girl with a plan, but God had changed everything. My plans for my life seemed to trail behind me like the remnants of popped balloons. I'd blown my chance with journalism, which was fine with me; I didn't want to do it anymore anyway. But I didn't have anything to replace it. I had no idea what part was mine to play in the world. I was different, I was new, but I didn't know what my different, new self was supposed to do with my life. I needed a hint, a direction, something.

"God what do you want me to do with my life?" I barely whispered into the quiet room.

As I lay there, staring at my feet pressed on the bunk above me, a sentence came to my mind, or rather hit me square in the face.

Write a book called The Lipstick Gospel.

Epilogue: Anything But Boring

I don't know how you came to pick up this book. I don't know what your experience with God or church or Christians has been. Maybe you've been a Christian all your life, maybe you're like me and you've never considered it. But whoever you are and wherever you come from, I want you to know how much God loves you. He does. It's hard to believe. I have to remind myself all the time, but He does.

He doesn't love you because you're shined up or perfect or because your church attendance is impeccable or because you are a decently good person. He loves you because He loves you. He loves you the way He loves me—messy and stinky and not looking for Him at all.

We all have reasons and ideas that keep us away from God. I definitely did. But I finally came to a place where I'd lived my life to the best of my ability and had come to the end of my rope. Maybe you've found yourself there too.

Whether you've been a Christian forever or for thirty seconds or never ever in your life, I truly believe God has an awesome plan in mind for you. It's not going to be easy, and you may get a little dirty along the way, but it's good—better than your own idea for your life, I'd bet.

I know because I've experienced it.

Life with God is wilder than the wildest roller coaster ride, and safer than your childhood bedroom. It's more thrilling than the greatest adventure, and more delicious than an Italian cappuccino—if you can even believe it.

He's just waiting for us to go all in—for us to cut the rope that's been keeping us at the dock, and for us to trust Him with our map. And when we do that, when we go all in, letting Him navigate, we'll go places that are so amazing, we wouldn't believe them even if we were told.